Anonymous

Bye Laws of the Constituent Synagogues

Anonymous

Bye Laws of the Constituent Synagogues

ISBN/EAN: 9783337232986

Printed in Europe, USA, Canada, Australia, Japan

Cover: Foto ©Suzi / pixelio.de

More available books at **www.hansebooks.com**

ק״ק כנסת ישראל

UNITED SYNAGOGUE.

———◆———

BYE LAWS

OF THE

CONSTITUENT SYNAGOGUES.

———◆———

PUBLISHED BY AUTHORITY OF THE COUNCIL OF
THE UNITED SYNAGOGUE:
OFFICE: 2, CHARLOTTE STREET, PORTLAND PLACE,
LONDON.

———◆———

חשון תרמ״ב,
NOVEMBER, 1881.

LONDON:
WERTHEIMER, LEA & CO., PRINTERS,
CIRCUS PLACE, LONDON WALL.

INTRODUCTION.

GREAT SYNAGOGUE.

PREFACE

TO THE EDITION OF THE LAWS PUBLISHED IN 5517—1827.

" The Wardens of the Great Synagogue, Duke's Place, presume
" that it will neither be deemed irrelevant nor intrusive, if they
" seize the opportunity afforded by the publication and distribu-
" tion of the newly arranged Code of Laws, to prefix to the same
" an account of the early establishment of this Congregation,
" together with a cursory detail of its present arrangement, and
" of the course pursued by the Officers and Vestry to effect the
" objects of their anxious care.

" It appears, from the remnant of an ancient manuscript book
" of laws and minutes of transactions, still existing among the
" documents lying in the Synagogue Chambers, that a meeting
" for prayer at least, if not a place specially devoted for Public
" Worship, must have been established by the German Jews
" prior to the year תנ״ב לפ״ק or 1692 : the Synagogue in Duke's
" Place, however, was the first building (excepting that of the
" Portuguese Congregation), purposely erected for divine service
" after their settlement in this happy realm in the year 1655.
" This pious work was effected at the sole expense of Moses
" Hart, Esq., a wealthy merchant of that time, the consecration
" of which took place on the Eve of the New Year ר״ה תפ״ב לפ״ק
" A.M. 5482 or 1722; and, by a codicil to the will of this
" religious and generous benefactor, bearing date 1756, the pro-
" perty was bequeathed to the Congregation altogether.

" In תקכ״ז or 1767, this Building was repaired, enlarged, and
" consecrated. Since that period, however, the community having
" greatly increased, the whole was taken down and the present
" elegant structure (being twice the size of the former) was
" erected in תק״נ or 1790; toward the expense of which, Mrs.
" Judith Levy, the then only surviving daughter of the original
" founder, subscribed the sum of £4,000.

" The Synagogue thus renewed, is the oldest and most spacious
" in London belonging to the German Jews; besides which, as
" the population has increased, several others have since been
" erected; but, in consequence of its early standing, this of
" Duke's Place has always been the principal point whereto the
" poor, both resident and foreign, have looked for, and found
" relief. At the head of its religious department, we have, at
" the present time, the happiness to boast of the superintendence
" of the highly-gifted and worthy Dr. SOLOMON HIRSCHEL,
" Q.D.C., whose reverend and esteemed father also guided Israel
" in this place from the year חק"ז or 1757 to תקכ"ד or 1764;
" divine worship is, of course, regularly and devoutly attended
" to under his auspices, while the Honorary Officers and Vestry
" are zealously employed in the general superintendence, in the
" dispensation of charity to the poor, the attention to the sick,
" and burial of the dead. Fixed monthly stipends are allotted to
" proper objects as well as casual relief administered as occa-
" sions arise, and the sums dispensed among the foreign poor
" who apply are very considerable, besides a large annual expense
" incurred for the distribution of מצות for which there always are
" an immense number of applicants; a Physician, Surgeon, and
" Apothecary are also engaged to attend in their several depart-
' ments for the benefit of the poor.

" Thus are our principal duties, of worship to the Almighty
" God, and charity to his creatures, attempted to be fulfilled.
" May we find grace in the sight of the Lord, and may he bless
" his people ! AMEN.

" It must be evident, that an establishment like this, requires
" very large funds to effect its purposes; and the managers have
" the satisfaction to declare, that the Congregation has met with
" many liberal supporters, and the poor with many generous
" friends. Several large sums have been settled in the funds,
" and their produce confided to the management of the Vestry
" for specific charitable purposes, to be annually distributed;
" and the names of LAZARUS SIMONS, Esq., ISRAEL ELKIN,
" Esq., of Jamaica, and ASHER GOLDSMID, Esq., must, on this
" account, be particularly noticed, while the enumeration of the
" rest of the generous benefactors to the Congregation, is in this
" place impossible; their names are justly inscribed in golden
" letters on the tablets in the synagogue, and their deeds are
" registered in Heaven.

" Such liberality is as honourable to the donors as it is indis-

" pensable to the Congregation, as, but for the generosity of the
" public, the Jewish Poor would be very badly provided for ;
" parochial relief being principally given in workhouses, our in-
" digent brethren are consequently deprived of such assistance ;
" and, although in France, Holland, Hamburgh, &c., the law of
" the land authorises the Jewish Congregations to levy a rate
" on their brethren for their Synagogue establishment and the
" maintenance of their poor, the laws of England do not permit
" a compulsory tax to be raised by any separate community with-
" out a special act of Parliament ; hence, the only resource and
" hope of this Congregation rest on the voluntary contributions
" of its members, nor is this hope groundless ; for the Jews are
" by all acknowledged to be compassionate and charitable, being
" fully impressed with the words of scripture :—

כי לא יחדל אביון מקרב הארץ על כן אנכי מצוך לאמר פתח
תפתח את ידך לאחיך לעניך ולאבינך בארצך · נתן תתן לו ולא
ירע לבבך בתתך לו כי בגלל הדבר הוה יברכך ה׳ אלהיך בכל
מעשיך ובכל משלח ידך :

דברים ט״ו י״א י׳

" The poor shall never cease out of the land : therefore I
" command thee, saying, Thou shalt open wide thine hand unto
" thy brother, to thy poor, and to thy needy, in thy land. Thou
" shalt surely give him, and thine heart shall not be grieved when
" thou givest unto him : because that for this thing the Lord thy
" God shall bless thee in all thy works, and in all that thou
" puttest thine hand unto."—*Deut.* chap. xv. verses 11 and 10.

" The Congregation have hitherto been highly benefited by
" the bequests of pious and benevolent persons, among which
" may be mentioned those from the late MOSES HART, Esq.,
" Founder of the Synagogue, ISAAC FRANKS, Esq., AARON
" FRANKS, Esq., Dr. SAMUEL DE FALK, LEVY BARENT COHEN,
" Esq., JUDAH PHILLIPS, Esq., of Jamaica, DANIEL ELIASON,
" Esq., and many others, besides settled funds for peculiar pur-
" poses as heretofore mentioned."

Extract from the Preface to the Edition of the same Laws,
published in 5623—1863.

IN 1854, "there having been no reprint of the Laws since the
" years 5587—1827, and many of them then in existence having
" been subsequently abrogated, or modified, and several new

" Laws enacted, the Committee of the Congregation determined
" to submit to the consideration of the Vestry the desirability of
" a revised code.

" Pursuant to a resolution of the Committee, passed at a
" Meeting held on the 7th November, 5615—1854, and ratified
" by a resolution of the Vestry at a Meeting held on the 23rd
" of the same month, a Sub-Committee was appointed to draw
" up such revised code.   The Sub-Committee was constituted as
" follows :

" Dr. BARNARD VAN OVEN,	SAMUEL MOSES, Esq.
" *Chairman.*	JOSHUA ALEXANDER, Esq.
" LOUIS NATHAN, Esq.	SAMPSON SAMUEL, Esq.
" LEWIS JACOBS, Esq.	MAURICE SOLOMON, Esq.

" It is only a duty to the memory of the respected Chairman
" of the Sub-Committee, to quote the concluding paragraph of
" the report in question :—

" ' The Committee cannot close this Report without recording
" ' their grateful appreciation of the eminent services of their
" ' esteemed Chairman, Dr. VAN OVEN, who has invariably
" ' attended every Meeting, and whose talents, experience, and
" ' urbanity, have greatly aided the Committee in their attempt
" ' to adequately fulfil the trust confided to them.'

" The Sub-Committee, in their Report, state that they com-
" menced their labours on the 24th January, 5615—1855, that
" they elected the Secretary of the Synagogue, Mr. SIMEON
" OPPENHEIM, an Honorary Member, and that his complete
" knowledge of the present Laws, and the manner of their
" operation, had been of the greatest value to the Sub-Committee
" at each step of their proceedings.

" The Revised Code was submitted to the consideration of the
" Vestry, and underwent the most careful and minute considera-
" tion of that body, during a series of Meetings ranging over a
" period of nearly three years.   With such modifications as were
" made by the Vestry, it was then, conformably to Law, sub-
" mitted to the consideration of the conjoint body of the Vestry
" and forty-two Members, and recommended for their adoption ;
" such portions of the same as relate to religious matters having
" previously been submitted to the consideration of the Chief
" Rabbi, the Rev. Dr. ADLER.

"The present revised Code has thus been prepared with much
"care ; and is framed not only to meet the requirements of the
"present time, but also in strict accordance with those principles
"which have hitherto governed the Congregation, and to which
"pious reference is made in the original Preface.

"It may be interesting generally to note, how importantly,
"since the date of the last promulgated code, the Great Syna-
"gogue has advanced in the wide extent of its religious influ-
"ences, and in the increased amount of its benefactions ; and
"how, by the establishment of a Branch Synagogue in Great
"Portland Street, it has been enabled to meet the requirements
"of its Members, whom the habits of the present time have
"located at a distance from the original building.

"In the First Preface, a just and glowing tribute is paid to
"the efficiency of the then Chief Rabbi, the late Dr. SOLOMON
"HIRSCHEL, ל"צז"ל ; and it is a source of the highest gratifica-
"tion at the present time to testify how much the Congregation
"and the Jewish community at large are indebted for their
"spiritual welfare, to the learning, zeal, and ability of the present
"Chief Rabbi, the Rev. Dr. N. M. ADLER ; and it is considered
"that this Introduction cannot be better concluded, than by the
"expression of the fervent prayer, that, under God's blessing,
"the Chief Rabbi may be long spared to continue in the exercise
"of his sacred functions; and, that, under the like blessing, the
"Great Synagogue may be enabled adequately to provide for the
"religious requirements of its increasing Congregation, so that
"the parent Synagogue and its branches may at all times find
"that the liberality of their Congregants is keeping pace with
"the increasing demand on their financial resources."

HAMBRO' SYNAGOGUE.

EXTRACT FROM THE INTRODUCTION
TO THE EDITION OF THE LAWS PUBLISHED IN 5605—1844.

"CONCORD, which is the foundation of social happiness, is only
"to be preserved by the adoption of such regulations as are con-
"ducive to the general welfare.

" Laws are therefore necessary for the establishment of good
" order; and that the same may be preserved, it is necessary that
" we implicitly observe such Laws framed for the support and
" benefit of the Congregation.

" The inefficiency of Laws to regulate our Congregation has
" been long felt by those who have had the management of its
" affairs; for although all those laid down for religious ob-
" servances are clearly deduced from sacred sources, yet the
" government of Assemblies for the worship of God, requires
" certain rules and orders to be followed, in order that the eccen-
" tricity of individuals may not disturb the general harmony.
" Besides the regulations requisite for the procurance of funds
" to defray the current expenditure of the establishment, and
" charitable dispensations to the poor always attached thereto ;
" as it must be evident that an establishment of this description
" requires funds to effect its purposes; and the Managers
" have the satisfaction to declare that the Congregation has
" met with very liberal supporters, and the poor with many
" generous friends. Several sums have been settled in the funds,
" and their produce confided to the management of the Committee
" for specific charitable purposes, to be annually distributed in
" Coals, Great Coats, &c., and the names of E. P. Salomons, Esq.
" (who bequeathed the Synagogue to this Congregation), Abra-
" ham Salomons, Esq., and Solomon Abrahams, Esq., must on
" this account be particularly noticed. While the enumeration of
" the rest of the general benefactors to the Congregation is in this
" place impossible, their names are justly inscribed in golden
" letters on the tablets in the Synagogue. Prayers are read for
" the repose of their souls at the specially appointed times, and
" their deeds are without doubt registered in Heaven.

וְיִהְיוּ לְרָצוֹן אִמְרֵי פִינוּ וְהֶגְיוֹן לִבֵּנוּ לְפָנֶי יְיָ צוּרֵנוּ וְגוֹאֲלֵנוּ

" And may the words of our mouths and the meditations of our
" hearts be acceptable in thy presence, O Lord, who art our
" Rock and Redeemer.

" Attempts have, however, at various times been made to
" supply this want of efficient Laws and Regulations, but from
" a variety of causes they have uniformly failed of being
" completed."

NEW SYNAGOGUE.

EXTRACT FROM THE PREFACE

TO THE EDITION OF THE LAWS PUBLISHED IN 5612—1851.

" EVERY nation and every community is governed by laws ; they
" are requisite for its constitution, the establishing of good order,
" and the well-being of society ; the effluxion of time also ren
" ders it necessary that there should be occasional alterations and
" modifications of those laws, so as to meet the reforms and
" improvements which the advancement of our social, moral, and
" religious positions demand.

" All law originates from intuitive principles of responsibility
" to Justice fixed in the Human Mind by DIVINE WISDOM ; the
" world is governed by it, whilst every class, every collective
" body, and every division of the created universe, has its own
" specific Laws, each forming part of a fundamental whole, the
" law of morality being one of its chief features. This is a great
" principle, by means of which, the world of life attains its pro-
" gression—it is the axis, upon which the whole of Human
" Existence revolves, it is the root from which all the branches
" of the Tree of Knowledge spread and extend their influence in
" every direction, wherever reason and judgment assist its
" sway.

" The Law of Morality is undoubtedly coeval with, or had its
" origin in, the Mosaic Code, called forth by all the mental
" qualifications of our great Lawgiver, from the Divine ideas
" implanted by the Creator for the moral and religious guidance
" of the whole human race. This Code of Law has continued
" in force to the present day, aided by numerous contingent and
" tributary forms, harmonizing with the general principles, upon
" which they were grafted ; but as time alters the condition of
" all things, so their subsidiary regulations require also some
" additional particulars for our government ; and it is for this

" reason, that the Elders of our Congregation, with such Mem-
" bers as were willing to undertake the task, were appointed a
" Committee, for the revising, amending, and making such
" additional Laws, as they should find necessary, for the
" protection of good government, and the endeavouring to
" preserve intact our Holy Religion, with a strict adherence to
" the dispensation of the Law, as written in the sacred volume,
" which the Committee have laboured to set forth ; for the obser-
" vance, and they trust, for the more efficient regulation of our
" pious and worthy Congregation."

PREFACE.

THE Council of the United Synagogue, in publishing
the Laws and Bye-Laws of its Constituent Synagogues, considers it desirable to prefix thereto a
short summary of the communal organisation which
existed prior to its establishment, with a narrative
of the proceedings connected with its foundation,
and a sketch of the principal measures which have
since occupied its attention.

The preface to the Laws of the Great Synagogue,
printed above, gives a short account of the foundation
of that Synagogue.

The Hambro' and New Synagogues were both
offshoots from the Great Synagogue, but their interests were considered to be so divergent, that
originally they declined to be governed, even in
spiritual affairs, by the same ecclesiastical authorities.
Each Synagogue had its own Rabbinical Chief, exercising authority over his own congregants, and en-
joying independent jurisdiction. So fearful was each

Congregation of the increase of Synagogues, to the injury of its own exchequer, that each Code of Laws contained rigorous provisions against the assemblage of its members in private meetings for prayer, and heavy fines were levied from those who ventured to disregard this prohibitory legislation.

The first advance towards conjoint action was effected in 5518—1758, when the Great and Hambro' Synagogues appointed one Chief Rabbi, with ecclesiastical jurisdiction over both Congregations. But it was not for many years that any further progress in this direction was attempted.

The next recorded endeavour was made by the late Chief Rabbi, the Rev. Dr. Solomon Hirschel. His earnest labours resulted, in the year 5565—1805, in the formation of a compact between the Great, Hambro' and New Synagogues, for the purposes of charity. So important did he deem this event, that he presented to each of the contracting bodies a congratulatory ode in Hebrew and English verse. The copy presented to the Great Synagogue, and which is still preserved in its vestry room, states that the presentation was made "to the vestries of the three Synagogues after the adjustment of the differences between them, and their conclusive arrangement respecting the united care of the strange poor in London."

In the same year another considerable step was taken towards ensuring concerted action among the London Jewish Congregations. There had existed for many years a Committee of the Spanish and Portuguese Congregation, charged with the duty of communicating with the Government on all questions concerning Acts of Parliament and other laws specially affecting the Jews. This Committee, after much discussion, agreed to co-operate with a similar Committee appointed by the Great Synagogue; and in the year 1760 these two sections of British Jews resolved mutually to communicate to each other any public affair which might become known to one of them, and which might interest "the two *nations*." The next step was in 1789, when delegates from the Great, Hambro' and New Synagogues attended the meetings of the Portuguese "Deputados," but for the purpose of consultation only. In 1805, however, by the invitation of the Deputies, all the Jewish Congregations of Great Britain were requested to send representatives to join "in all transactions that may concern us as one body." The Board of Deputies, consisting of these representatives, received Parliamentary recognition in 1836 for the purpose of certifying Secretaries for the Registration of Marriages under the Act passed in that year.

The treaty or compact between the three City German Congregations, already alluded to, continued in force till 5594—1834, when there were published the articles of a new treaty agreed to by the Sub-Committees of the Great, Hambro' and New Synagogues. In this new compact the scope of concerted action was much enlarged, and it was agreed that various communal duties, both religious and charitable, should be discharged in common, the cost of the same being defrayed in the proportions of one moiety by the Great Synagogue, and one-fourth part each by the

New and Hambro' Synagogues. Each Synagogue
was precluded from accepting as a member anyone
attached to either of the other contracting Synagogues, or even from letting a seat to anyone so
attached, and any contributions received, even inadvertently, in violation of this agreement, were to
be handed over to the Synagogue to which the contributor was considered to belong.

An arrangement of this kind, which worked without
inconvenience when the congregants of each Synagogue were grouped round their respective places of
worship, became at times somewhat oppressive when
they removed to various parts of the metropolis, and
necessarily attended the Synagogues which gradually
became established in the districts in which they
resided. For example, in the Portland Street Branch
of the Great Synagogue, a member of another Synagogue could only obtain a seat with the permission
of the executive of his own Synagogue, and could
not take any part in the management ; while, as
regards privileges, he occupied his seat under a totally
different tenure to that of his neighbours.

An inconvenience still graver than this was felt
in the City Synagogues themselves; a majority of
the members constituting the Boards of Management no longer attended the places of worship which
they controlled; and the anomaly therefore existed
that in the East end of London, where the chief
seat of government still remained, the affairs were
mainly regulated by gentlemen who did not worship
at the sacred buildings to whose wants they administered; while, on the other hand, the affairs of

the Western Branches were regulated from the Central Office in the City.

The patience of the members, and the harmony and good feeling of the officers of the various Synagogues, greatly mitigated the effect of the anomalies which, under the altered condition of the Jews as to residence, had arisen from the treaty. It might even have been practicable to uphold that system for a short time longer, but several circumstances combined to impress on the Executives of the Synagogues the expediency of introducing the inevitable change while the majority of the community were still attached to the old religious centres, by ties of allegiance, affection, or inheritance.

The most important of these circumstances was the establishment of Synagogues in the extreme west, in the north and in the south of London, and the position which they assumed :—

1. In the extreme west, at Bayswater, the precedent of the Portland Street Branch was followed as far as possible ; but, for the first time, it was found necessary to appoint honorary officers and a committee apart from the parent bodies, with limited powers of legislation and of control over the income and expenditure, subject to the veto of the parent Synagogues. The accidental circumstance of the principal members of this Branch Synagogue having seats at the parent Boards, prevented, at the time, any grave inconvenience from this arrangement ; but it was manifest that when this tie lapsed, a natural consequence in the course of years, it would be difficult to reconcile the members of this and of other

Synagogues which might hereafter be similarly established, to the fact that being unrepresented at the parent Boards, they would have but a limited control over the administration of the funds which they contributed.

2. In the north of London a Synagogue had been built, the connection of which with the parent Synagogues was still more slight than at Bayswater, nothing but a poll tax being contributed to retain membership, and the income and expenditure being totally free from any of the recognised communal burdens borne by the older bodies.

3. In the south of London a Synagogue had been erected which had no connexion whatever with the parent bodies. Nothing was contributed from their funds to the cost of its erection, and though its members were mainly members of the older bodies, they contributed to the latter only just sufficient to retain the right of burial in the Cemeteries.

The financial prospect of the parent Synagogues thus gave rise to serious apprehensions. Deprived of the contributions of their wealthier members, who . were all leaving them for more favoured districts, the burden of ministering to the various ecclesiastical, religious and charitable requirements incidental to the religion, remained with them, while the means of maintenance visibly diminished, and the ties of allegiance from their former members became weaker year by year.

Even these considerations of membership and finance, important as they had become, might still have been disregarded, if it had been found that the discharge of duties more sacred in their nature was efficiently provided for under the old system, and would be endangered by a new one. But on the contrary, the want of improved administration in the management of the burial grounds, in attendance on the sick·and the dying, in the supervision of the poor, and in attention to the requirements of the sanitary and dietary laws, was patent to all who took part in the management of the affairs of the community.

Thus it will be seen that every consideration, religious, social and financial, alike pointed to a reconstruction of the bond of union which had hitherto kept the Congregations in some measure together ; it was not therefore surprising that an accidental and undesigned circumstance served to bring about a movement for which every mind appeared so fully prepared.

This incident was supplied by the resistance of two members of one of the contracting Synagogues, who having been some years previously inadvertently accepted by another Synagogue, declined to resume the membership of the one to which they had originally belonged. A conference ensued between the Executives of the Great and New Synagogues on the point, and the discussion took the shape not only of redressing the inadvertent breach of treaty which had taken place, but of endeavouring to prevent the possibility of a similar occurrence in the future. With the view of ensuring so desirable a consummation, the Rev. Dr. Nathan M. Adler, Chief Rabbi, suggested to and impressed on the Wardens of the Great Synagogue, assembled round his table on the morning of the first day of the Feast of Tabernacles, 5627—1866, the advisability of endeavouring to unite the Congregations under one management. The honorary officers of the Great and New Synagogues already delegated, invited the co-operation of the honorary officers of the Hambro' Synagogue, and in the subsequent month of November each body of officers submitted to their respective Boards the general question of an amalgamation. These Boards passed resolutions approving the desirability and affirming in substance the principle of an amalgamation, and appointed delegates to confer and prepare a scheme to be submitted to them for approval.

Delegates from the Bayswater Synagogue were subsequently invited and appointed; and after many meetings, extending over some time, a scheme which received the sanction of the Chief Rabbi was prepared by the delegates, and recommended by them to the various Synagogues for adoption.

The scheme endeavoured to unite the members of the Synagogues generally into one great Congregation, having one common interest, governed by one fundamental code of laws, and capable of embracing every kindred Metropolitan Congregation in one bond of membership, while at the same time strengthening the feeling of local interest and attachment necessary for promoting the welfare and success of the several Synagogues. The scheme secured for every member unfettered discretion in the selection of his place of worship, and gave to every seatholder a voice in the election of those who were to perform the services, to control the finances, and to direct the affairs of his synagogue.

The scheme underwent some modifications, but all its main features were adopted by the Boards of Management of the Great, Hambro', New and Bayswater Synagogues, and it was submitted for the approval and ratification of the members at General Meetings held at the respective Synagogues on April 19, 5628—1868. At these meetings the scheme for the Union of the Synagogues was, with certain modifications, approved, and authority was given to the Boards of Management to take the necessary steps for carrying it into effect. Many of the recommendations which were adopted, and especially those proposing to deal with the trusts and endowments of the Constituent Synagogues, required the sanction of the Charity Commissioners for England and Wales, to whom application was consequently made. After the necessary investigation by the Commissioners, the scheme, translated into legal phraseology, was incorporated in the Seventeenth Report of the Commissioners, dated February 26, 1870, was then presented by them to Parliament, and on the 14th July, 1870, the "Act for Confirming a scheme of the Charity Commissioners for the Jewish United Synagogues" (33 and 34 Vict., Ch. cxvi.) received the Royal Assent and became part of the law of the land.

The Hebrew title, ק״ק כנסת ישראל, that was felicitously chosen for the Amalgamated Body, is one fraught with great and solemn reminiscences. It embodies aspirations for unity, harmony, and

concord in the future, together with recollections of
a great, glorious, and imperishable past. May it
typify results commensurate with the feelings of
which it is the symbol!

———

In the decade that has elapsed since the foundation
of the United Synagogue, many important measures
for the amelioration of the religious and social condition of the Community have been adopted, and
many additions rendered necessary by its rapid aug-
mentation and development have been sanctioned. It
may, indeed, be affirmed that in every department of
communal life, the awakened attention attracted to
communal affairs, and the benefits of a unified and
concentrated administration, soon became apparent, as
will be amply evidenced by the following short summary of the work of the past few years.

At the first meeting of the Council it was resolved
to embody in a declaration of trust, equally binding
on any Congregations in the Union with the Act
of Parliament itself, all those clauses which the
Charity Commissioners had eliminated as being un-
suitable for parliamentary legislation. These clauses
referred to the maintenance of the Chief Rabbi and
the Ecclesiastical Board, to the control of the Chief
Rabbi over matters connected with the religious
administration of the United Synagogue, and to the
imposition of pecuniary penalties in certain special
cases.

The endowments and trusts were soon after placed

under the control of a Special Committee, which has efficiently administered the varied and responsible duties entrusted to it, while the distribution of the Synagogue Charity has at the same time been economically and wisely directed under the machinery prescribed by the Act itself.

The Council has also assumed the duty previously undertaken by the Committee for the diffusion of Religious knowledge, namely, the visitation of all public institutions containing Jewish inmates, such as Hospitals, Prisons, Reformatories, Workhouses, and Lunatic Asylums. This work, which requires much delicacy and tact, is under the superintendance of a Committee specially appointed, and is carried out with great ability and intelligence not only by the ministers of the Constituent Synagogues, but also by ministers of other Metropolitan and Provincial Synagogues, and occasionally by laymen. A special fund was instituted for the relief of discharged patients, prisoners, &c., to which the United Synagogue contributes, and this comprehensive work, which has almost grown to the limits of an ordinary special institution, shows how potent for good a combined and unified administration can speedily become.

The whole of the marriage regulations of the different Congregations have been revised and harmonised. Facilities have been given for the celebration of marriages at merely nominal rates, and the excuse formerly pleaded for immorality and irregular celebration of marriages, namely, the high charge made by the Synagogues, has been entirely removed. Education has not been neglected. The Beth Hamidrash has been affiliated to the United Synagogue, and a competent gentleman appointed to give instruction in Hebrew and Rabbinical Literature in the English language. A considerable sum has been for some years annually voted to the Jews' College for the training of Jewish ministers. Funds at the same time have been largely contributed towards the erection and foundation of Synagogues in such districts of London as required them. A new Cemetery has been purchased at the extreme west of London, towards the cost of which large voluntary contributions were received, and additional land was purchased for the Cemetery at the extreme east, the cost of which fell exclusively on the Communal funds.

At the same time that additions were thus made to the responsibilities of the United Synagogue, and that new properties were acquired in fresh districts, the older Synagogues were not forgotten. In each of the City Synagogues various ground charges existed which have been redeemed, and all the older Synagogues have been completely renovated and restored since the Union took place.

While the Council thus gave evidence of life and energy, the members of the different Synagogues showed an increasing attention to Communal affairs. The annual elections for Honorary Officers, Representatives and Committees, evoked a continuous interest on the part of the seatholders; this awakened vitality led to a desire for a revision of the distinction, which almost from time immemorial had existed among the members of a Synagogue, in their division into two classes, one of which was called בעלי בתים

(Privileged Members), and the other ordinary seat-holders. A first but very considerable step in the direction of the abolition of this distinction had been taken, at the time of the establishment of the United Synagogue, in the grant of a voice at all elections to all seatholders of twelve months' tenure, a right previously reserved to Privileged Members only. Experience having proved that the possession of the franchise aided in enlisting general interest in Communal objects, while in no degree lowering the character of the Representatives selected, it was not surprising that the policy of maintaining this distinction should be questioned. At several meetings of some Constituent Synagogues, the maintenance of Privileged membership was attacked, and the Council at length decided on submitting the question of its abolition to a meeting of delegates from all the Synagogues in conference with the Council, in the manner provided by one of the clauses of the scheme. The Council took the opportunity of introducing at this Conference various minor alterations in the scheme which they had deemed to be advisable.

The Conference was held on May 24th, 5640—1880, under the presidency of Sir N. M. de Rothschild, Bart., M.P., the President of the United Synagogue, and it was resolved that " no Privileged Member shall be made " after that date. Due provision was at the same time made for preserving all the existing rights of present Privileged Members, and for their preferential participation in the special Benevolent fund which existed for their benefit. The experience of the change is yet too recent for any authoritative opinion to be given as to its consequences, but as far as any appearances to the contrary can be discerned, no fears are now entertained as to the result of the effacement of distinctions that had already become shadowy.

Under the provisions of the United Synagogues Act, the various Constituent Synagogues continued, after the Union, to be administered under the same laws and regulations which had previously governed them. These were supplemented from time to time by new laws initiated by the Council, or suggested by the Boards of Management of the different Congregations for its sanction. Certain changes were also made, founded upon resolutions of the Council, and the natural operation of the new system at the same time tended to make many of the old laws either obsolete or inoperative. It was at length found indispensable to authorise the preparation of a new Code, embodying the laws then in existence, with the introduction of such changes as might be found desirable. This authority was given by resolution of Council on November 3rd, 1874, and it was determined to proceed in the first instance with the preparation of those laws which are denominated in the Act "Bye-laws," and which govern the constitution and proceedings of the Constituent Synagogues, as distinguished from those laws which have no special local significance. It is provided in the Act that these Bye-laws should be submitted by the Boards of Management of the Constituent Synagogues for the approval of the Council. The duty of preparing the Code was entrusted by the Council to the Executive

Committee, in conjunction with the Local Boards
of Management; but the merit of the detailed work
incidental to the composition of the Code must be
ascribed to a Sub-committee, which consisted of three
Members of the Executive Committee of the United
Synagogue, and of two Delegates selected by each
Board of Management from its own Members. Mr.
Lionel L. Cohen was appointed Chairman of the
Delegates, who were engaged for some years in the
preparation of their arduous task, which was temporarily interrupted while the question of the maintenance or abolition of the Privileged Membership
was under consideration.

In this manner the present Code was gradually
formulated. When the Bye-laws had been framed by
the Delegates, they were transmitted to the respective
Boards of Management for their approval and revision,
and then finally passed by the Council. The framers
had kept in view the exigencies of each Synagogue as
embodied in their then existing laws and customs,
and where no material principle was involved, it has
not been thought necessary to insist on absolute uni-
formity of legislation in each Congregation. The
framers of the Code have rather endeavoured to
secure general harmony, and it will be found that
the differences of enactment which exist in the
various Synagogues are trivial, and such as will entail
no inconvenience on members who may remove from
one Synagogue to another. These Bye-laws, "slowly
broadening down from precedent to precedent," are
not the result of hasty or spasmodic legislation; they
are the outcome of deliberate growth and of the most

careful consideration of the requirements of the Community.

In the preparation of the Code of Laws the Delegates were favoured by the able assistance of Mr. Morris S. Oppenheim and of Mr. Algernon E. Sydney, the Hon. Solicitor to the Council ; the legal experience of these gentlemen in the different branches of their profession was of great service to the Delegates, and the labour expended by them, in giving precision to the phraseology of the Laws, and in reconciling their different provisions, merits the warmest appreciation. The duty of preparing the present code of Laws for publication was entrusted to Messrs. Lionel L. Cohen, Noah Davis, and Maurice Hart, who were efficiently assisted by Dr. A. Asher, the Secretary to the Council of the United Synagogue.

The Delegates had the satisfaction of receiving the sanction of the Rev. the Chief Rabbi, Dr. Nathan Marcus Adler to the work in which they were engaged. For thirty-six years Dr. Adler has served the Jewish Community as their spiritual Chief, and it is a source of gratification to repeat in the Preface to these Laws, adapted to the requirements of the United Synagogues, the tribute of veneration, regard and affection paid to Dr. Adler in the Preface to the Laws of the Great Synagogue eighteen years ago. May he long be spared, by the Divine Blessing, to continue in the exercise of his sacred functions!

This sketch of the circumstances which gradually culminated in the amalgamation of the Synagogues, and which have since characterised the brief history of the United body, would be incomplete did it not record the names of the gentlemen originally appointed by the Synagogues as Delegates for the purpose of preparing the scheme which formed the basis of the United Synagogues' Act. Many of them have not been spared to see the fruition of their labours, while others continue to render to the Congregation zealous and invaluable service, advancing the interests of the Community which owes them so much, and of which their talents and public spirit have long constituted them distinguished ornaments. They were as follows :—

Delegates from the Great Synagogue.—Sir Anthony Rothschild, Bart., Messrs. Lionel Louis Cohen, Jacob Waley, M.A., Hyam Leopold Beddington, Joseph Lazarus, Moses Symons, Louis Nathan, Joshua Alexander, Sampson Samuel, Simeon Oppenheim and Lewis Jacobs. On the death of Mr. Sampson Samuel, Ald. Sir Benjamin S. Phillips was chosen in his stead.

Hambro' Synagogue.—Messrs. Henry Aaron Isaacs, Moses Van Praagh, Hyam Levy, Isaac A. Boss, Jonas Engel, Moses Solomon Keyser, Joseph M. Isaacs and Lewis Lyons. On the death of Mr. Jonas Engel his son, Mr. Lawrence Engel, was appointed in his stead.

New Synagogue.—Messrs. Henry Solomon, Philip Salomons, Marcus Samuel, Algernon Edward Sydney, Lawrence Levy, Sampson Lucas, Edward I. Sydney,

Noah Davis, Alexander Levy, and, on the death of
Mr. Philip Salomons, Mr. Solomon Schloss.

Bayswater Synagogue.—Messrs. Saul Isaac, David
Benjamin, Asher H. Hart, Samuel Montagu, Michael
Samuel and Joseph Levitt.

Mr. Lionel Louis Cohen was unanimously elected
Chairman of the Delegates, and Dr. Asher Asher,
Secretary.

As soon as the Council was constituted—in December, 1870—its first act was to appoint Sir Anthony
Rothschild, Bart., as President, and Messrs. Sampson
Lucas and Lionel L. Cohen, Vice-Presidents. Sir
Anthony Rothschild continued to serve the Council
in that capacity till his lamented death in January,
1876. His kindly and genial bearing, his great experience of Communal affairs, and his deep attachment to the Congregations over which he presided,
endeared him to all his colleagues, and enabled him
with comparative facility to organise that assembly
which he had materially helped to call into existence.
On his death Mr. Sampson Lucas, Vice-President,
was elected President, Sir Nathaniel M. de Rothschild, Bart., M.P., being appointed one of the Vice-
Presidents. Unfortunately, after a brief interval of
three years, the United Synagogue was again deprived
by death of the services of its President, an interval
far too short in the interest of the Institution which
Mr. Sampson Lucas had zealously served in many
capacities, but amply long enough to have secured to
him the affectionate regard of the Council over which
he had presided. Sir Nathaniel M. de Rothschild,
Bart., M.P., succeeded Mr. Lucas as President, the

vacant post of Vice-President being filled by the election of Baron Henry de Worms, M.P. Sir Nathaniel de Rothschild continues to fill the office of President, and vies with his predecessors in his attachment to the public service, on which he brings to bear unremitting attention, and the traditional devotion of his family to the advancement of the interests of the Congregation.

As the Synagogue is the centre of the spiritual and social life of the Community, and therefore necessarily interwoven with all its religious and domestic affairs, the laws framed for its guidance have necessarily a wide range. Their tendency should be to preserve the traditions of our Holy Religion, to uphold the dignity of the Community and the individuality of the various Synagogues, to place all members impartially on an equal footing, and to promote general concord. It is hoped that the present Code of Bye-laws fulfils these purposes, and that, as the United Synagogue is the expression of the unity and fraternal regard which should prevail among the individuals who in the aggregate form a Congregation, so may these Bye-laws be regarded as an indication of the stage of religious and social progress to which the Community as a whole has advanced. May the blessing of Our Father, so bountifully vouchsafed to His Children throughout their wanderings and dispersions, continue to rest on them, so that the work of their hands may ever redound to His Glory and to their honour. Amen.

Heshvan, 5642.
November, 1881.

UNITED SYNAGOGUE.

At the present time (5642—1881) the United Synagogue consists of Ten Constituent Synagogues, namely:—The Great, Hambro', New, Central, Bayswater, Boro', St. John's Wood, East London, North London, and West End Synagogues.

1. The present structure of the Great Synagogue was, as described in the foregoing preface to its laws, erected in 5550—1790 on the freehold site of a former Synagogue which bore the same name. A portion of the site, acquired for the reconstruction of the Synagogue in 1790, was held from the City of London on lease, renewable for ever on payment of a fine. The freehold of this portion was purchased from the Corporation of the City of London by the Council of the United Synagogue in 1874; and the whole of the site of the Great Synagogue and its appurtenances is therefore now freehold. The Synagogue contains 507 seats on the ground floor, and 231 in the gallery.

2. The Hambro' Synagogue, Church Row, Fenchurch Street, in the City of London, was originally founded in the year 5496—1736. The freehold of

the site and the existing building were bequeathed
to the Congregation in the year 1805 by Eleazar
Philip Salomons, Esq. The Synagogue contains 255
seats on the ground floor, and 135 in the gallery.

3. The NEW SYNAGOGUE was originally founded in
Leadenhall Street in the year 5520—1760. The
foundation stone of the present building in Great
St. Helen's, Bishopsgate Street, was laid by the late
Chief Rabbi, the Rev. Dr. Solomon Hirschel, on
ה' אייר תקצ"ז—May 10, 1837, and the Synagogue was
consecrated by him on כ"ג אלול תקצ"ח—Sept. 13,
1838. The site is freehold. The building contains
410 seats on the ground floor, and 152 in the gallery.

4. The CENTRAL SYNAGOGUE, in Great Portland
Street, was erected in lieu of the Branch Synagogue
which had been opened in the same street in April,
5615—1855. The site of the present building is
leasehold, and expires in 1967. The foundation stone
was laid by Baron Lionel de Rothschild, M.P., on
ו' ניסן תרכ"ט—March 18, 1869, and the Synagogue
was consecrated by the Rev. Dr. Nathan M. Adler,
Chief Rabbi, on ו' ניסן תר"ל—April 7, 1870, exactly
one year, by the Hebrew Calendar, from the laying of
the foundation stone, which date was also the anniversary of the consecration of the Great Synagogue and
of its Branch in Great Portland Street. The Central
Synagogue contains 461 seats on the ground floor,
and 364 in the gallery. The cost, inclusive of the
purchase of the leasehold interest, and of the
erection of two ministers' houses, was £37,284, of

which the sum of £22,884 was subscribed by the public, £6,000 was contributed by the United Synagogue, £7,800 was raised on debentures, now liquidated, and £600 was derived from the sale of life seats, etc.

5. The BAYSWATER SYNAGOGUE was founded in 5623—1863 as a branch of the Great and New Synagogues. The site is freehold. The foundation stone was laid by the Rev. Dr. Adler, on י״ב תמוז תרכ׳ב—July 10th, 1862, and the Synagogue was consecrated by him on י״ד אב תרכ׳ג—July 30th, 1863. There are 341 seats on the ground floor, and 334 in the gallery. The total cost of the Bayswater Synagogue, including site, decoration, and subsequent alterations in 1867, was £15,611. Of this amount £7,420 was contributed by the public, £3,000 was provided by the Parent bodies in equal proportions, and interest received on deposit account amounted to £380. The sum of £2,000 was borrowed from a Bank. No debentures were issued. From the opening of the Synagogue in 1863, the annual surplus income, after payment of rates to the Parent Synagogues, was allowed to accumulate, until, in 1870, it amounted to a sufficient sum for liquidating the deficit in the Building Account and for repaying the loan from the Bank.

The above five Synagogues constituted the United Synagogue at its foundation in 5640—1870. Of the other five Synagogues two have joined the United Synagogue since that date, and three have been founded under its auspices.

6. The BORO' SYNAGOGUE, the outcome of a private מנין held in the neighbourhood many years ago, was originally founded in St. George's-road, Southwark. The present building, which contains 206 seats on the ground floor, and 114 in the gallery, was consecrated by the Rev. Dr. Adler on ב' ניסן תרכ"ז —April 7, 1867, and the Synagogue joined the United Synagogue in 1873. The site is leasehold, the lease expiring in 1942. The building cost £4,800, defrayed by voluntary contributions and by a loan from a bank, subsequently repaid out of surplus income. This sum was exclusive of the cost of a school erected in connection with the Synagogue, but now separately administered.

7. The NORTH LONDON SYNAGOGUE joined the United Synagogue in 1878. The stone on which the Ark rests was laid by Baron Ferdinand de Rothschild on כ"ז כסלו תרכ"ח—December 24, 1867, the building being then near completion ; and the Synagogue was consecrated by the Rev. Dr. Adler, on ו' ניסן תרכ"ח— March 29, 1868, the anniversary by the Hebrew Calendar of the consecration of the Great and Central Synagogues. Its cost was £5,793, of which the sum of £4,183 was defrayed by voluntary contributions, £600 was raised by a loan on debentures, now liquidated, and £1,010 by an advance from the Great Synagogue. The site is leasehold, the lease expiring in 1964. There are 289 seats on the ground floor, and 231 in the gallery.

8. The ST. JOHN'S WOOD SYNAGOGUE, a temporary

iron building, was the first Synagogue founded under the auspices of the United Synagogue. The site is freehold. The cost of the site and temporary building was defrayed by voluntary contributions and by a vote of £1,000 made by the Council of the United Synagogue. There are 152 seats for gentlemen, and 90 seats for ladies. Authority for the foundation of the St. John's Wood Synagogue was given at a general meeting of the members of the United Synagogue, held on 13th July, 1876, and it was consecrated by the Rev. Dr. Adler, on כ׳ח אלול תרל׳ו—September 17, 5636. The building was opened free from debt. Arrangements are now in progress for the erection of a permanent edifice on the site of the temporary iron structure.

9. The EAST LONDON SYNAGOGUE was erected under the auspices of the United Synagogue, and the foundation stone was laid by Mr. Lionel Louis Cohen, on כ׳ג ניסן תרל׳ו—April 17, 1876. The site is freehold, and the Synagogue, which contains 314 seats on the ground floor, and 220 in the gallery, was consecrated by the Rev. Dr. Adler on י׳א ניסן תרל׳ז—March 25, 1877. The building was opened free from debt; the cost of the building and freehold site was £9,781, of which the sum of £2,000 was provided from the funds of the United Synagogue, and £7,781 raised by public subscription.

10. The WEST END SYNAGOGUE contains accommodation for 301 persons on the ground floor, and 278 in the gallery. The meeting of members of the United Synagogue, authorising its erection and ad-

mission into the Union, was held on May 10, 1877. The foundation stone was laid by Mr. Leopold de Rothschild, on כ״ז סיון תרל״ז—June 7, 1877, and the building was consecrated by the Rev. Dr. Adler on ׳י ניסן תרל״ט—March 30, 1879, the anniversary, by the Hebrew Calendar, of the consecration of the Great, Central and North London Synagogues. The cost, including the site, which will become freehold in about twenty-five years, was £24,980, of which the public contributed the sum of £13,297, £4,000 was provided from the funds of the United Synagogue, £6,500 was borrowed on Debenture, and the sale of life seats, &c., produced £1,183.

ק״ק כנסת ישראל

UNITED SYNAGOGUE.

CHIEF RABBI—Rev. Dr. Nathan Marcus Adler
DAYAN—Rev. Bernard Spiers.

PRESIDENT.

Sir Nathaniel M. De Rothschild, Bart., M.P.

VICE-PRESIDENTS.

Lionel L. Cohen, Esq. | Baron Henry de Worms, M.P.

TREASURERS.

David Davis, Esq. | Frederic M. Halford, Esq.

OVERSEERS OF THE POOR, AND TREASURERS OF THE BEQUESTS AND TRUSTS COMMITTEE.

Noah Davis, Esq. | Maurice Hart, Esq.

TREASURERS OF THE BURIAL SOCIETY.

Joseph Magnus, Esq. | Simon Simons, Esq.

LIST OF MEMBERS OF THE COUNCIL OF THE UNITED SYNAGOGUE.

Abrahams, H. A., Esq.
Abrahams, S., Esq.
Adler, Marcus N., Esq.
Alex, Ephraim, Esq.
Arnholtz, A., Esq.
Barnard, Daniel, Esq.
Barnett, Morris, Esq.
Beddington, A. H., Esq.
Beddington, Hyam L., Esq.
Beddington, Maurice, Esq.
Benjamin, David, Esq.
Benjamin, Joseph, Esq.
Benjamin, Moss, Esq.
Benjamin, M., Esq.

Bentwitch, M., Esq.
Berg, Ellis, Esq.
Bergtheil, J., Esq.
Birnbaum, B., Esq.
Bloomfield, R. Z., Esq.
Braunstein, N., Esq.
Cohen, Arthur B., Esq., Q.C., M.P.
Cohen, E. A., Esq.
Cohen, G., Esq.
Cohen, J. A., Esq.
Cohen, Lionel L., Esq.
Cohen, Louis, Esq.
Cohen, Neville D., Esq.

Collins, H. H., Esq.
Davidson, Louis, Esq.
Davis, Benn, Esq.
Davis, Charles, Esq.
Davis, Charles, Esq.
Davis, David, Esq.
Davis, Frederick, Esq.
Davis, J., Esq.
Davis, M., Esq.
Davis, Noah, Esq.
Ellis, Sir B. H., K.C.S.I.
Engel, Lawrence, Esq.
Flatau, A., Esq.
Flatau, William, Esq.
Franklin, Ellis A., Esq.
Friedlander, Albert, Esq.
Goldhill, John, Esq.
Graumann, E., Esq.
Halford, F. M., Esq.
Harris, J. M., Esq.
Harris, M., Esq.
Harris, M., Esq.
Harris, Samuel, Esq.
Hart, Henry, Esq.
Hart, James L., Esq.
Hart, Maurice, Esq.
Hyam, Lawrence, Esq.
Isaac, Saul, Esq.
Isaacs, Henry A., Esq.
Isaacs, Joseph M., Esq.
Israel, Henry A., Esq.
Jacobs, D. H., Esq.
Jacobs, D. L., Esq.
Jacobs, Harris, Esq.
Jacobs, John, Esq.
Jacobs, Judah, Esq.
Jacobs, Mark, Esq.
Jacobs, S., Esq.
Jonas, J. A., Esq.
Joseph, Isaac A., Esq.
Joseph, M. S., Esq.
Joseph, Nathan S., Esq.
Keyser, Assur, Esq.
Lazarus, Henry, Esq.

Lazarus, Lewis, Esq
Levy, Abraham, Esq.
Levy, Alexander, Esq.
Levy, Edward A., Esq.
Levy, H., Esq.
Levy, Lewis, Esq.
Levy, Moses, Esq.
Lion, A. J., Esq.
Lion, Lion, Esq.
Lucas, Edward, Esq.
Lucas, Henry, Esq.
Lyons, Lewis, Esq.
Maas, L., Esq.
Magnus, Joseph, Esq.
Marks, I. M., Esq.
Marsden, A. M., Esq.
Meyers, Barnett, Esq.
Montagu, Samuel, Esq.
Moses, Assur H., Esq.
Moses, Samuel, Esq.
Myers, A. N., Esq.
Myers, S., Esq.
Nathan, Louis, Esq.
Oppenheim, M. S., Esq.
Ososki, Louis, Esq.
Peartree, Henry, Esq.
Phillips, Sir B. S.
Phillips, L. H., Esq.
Pick, I., Esq.
Pool, Samuel, Esq.
Reubenson, Isidor, Esq.
Rosenfold, A., Esq.
Rothschild, Sir N. M. De,
 Bart, M.P.
Samuel, Charles, Esq.
Samuel, Stuart M., Esq.
Schloss, Sol., Esq.
Silber, A. M., Esq.
Silver, Solomon, Esq.
Simmonds, J. L., Esq.
Simons, Simon, Esq.
Solomon, Henry, Esq.
Solomon, Lewis, Esq.
Solomon, Saul, Esq.

Solomons, H. J., Esq.
Sydney, A. E., Esq.
Van Praagh, B. L., Esq.
Van Staveren, B., Esq.

Weingott, S., Esq.
Worms, Baron H. de, M.P.
Worms, Baron.

(Asher Asher, M.D., *Secretary*.)

SEVEN ELDERS.*

Benjamin, David, Esq.
Cohen, Lionel L., Esq.
Marks, I. M., Esq.
Samuel, Charles, Esq.

Solomon, Henry, Esq.
Solomon, Saul, Esq.
Worms, Baron Henry De, M.P.

* The above-named gentlemen, with the two Treasurers, the two Overseers of the Poor, and the Wardens of the Constituent Synagogues hereafter named, constitute the Executive Committee.

FINANCE COMMITTEE.

Arnholtz, A., Esq.
Benjamin, J., Esq.
Cohen, Neville D., Esq.
Israel, Henry A., Esq.
Joseph, Isaac A., Esq.

Lazarus, Henry, Esq.
Levy, Abraham, Esq.
Levy, Lewis, Esq.
Marks, I. M., Esq.
Weingott, S., Esq.

With the Treasurers.

OVERSEERS' COMMITTEE.

Alex, E., Esq.
Nathan, Louis, Esq.

Israel, Henry A., Esq.
Benjamin, David, Esq.

With the Overseers of the Poor.

BEQUESTS AND TRUSTS COMMITTEE.

Abrahams, H. A., Esq.
Berg, E., Esq.
Cohen, J. A. Esq.
Ellis, Sir B. H., K.C.S.I.
Jacobs, M., Esq.

Jacobs, S., Esq.
Jonas, J. A., Esq.
Levy, E. A., Esq.
Ososki, L., Esq.
Rosenfeld, A., Esq.

With the Treasurers, and the Overseers of the Poor and their Committee.

BUILDING COMMITTEE.

Samuel Montagu, Esq., *Chairman.*

Abrahams, Hyman A., Esq.
Beddington, Maurice H., Esq.
Bergtheil, J., Esq.
Collins, H. H., Esq.
Davis, David, Esq.
Flatau, W., Esq.
Harris, H. M., Esq.
Hart, Henry, Esq.
Israel, H. A., Esq.
Jacobs, John, Esq.
Jaffe, Martin, Esq.

Joseph, Isaac A., Esq.
Joseph, J. A., Esq.
Lazarus, R., Esq.
Levy, A., Esq.
Marks, I. M., Esq.
Myers, Mark, Esq.
Oppenheim, Morris S., Esq.
Silber, A. M., Esq.
Solomon, Saul, Esq.
Sydney, A. E., Esq.

REPRESENTATIVES AT THE CHIEF RABBI'S BOARD.

Alex, E., Esq.
Beddington, Hyam L., Esq.
Bergtheil, J., Esq.
Hymans, Henry, Esq.
Jacobs, John, Esq.
Jacobs, S., Esq.

Joseph, Morris S., Esq.
Levy, Hyam, Esq.
Moses, Sam., Esq.
Rosenfeld, Ab., Esq.
Solomon, Henry, Esq.

REPRESENTATIVES AT THE COUNCIL OF THE JEWS' COLLEGE.

Abrahams, Hyman A., Esq.
Davis, Benn, Esq.
Franklin, Ellis A., Esq.

Harris, Samuel, Esq.
Lucas, Edward, Esq.
Silber, A. M., Esq.

REPRESENTATIVES AT THE BOARD OF SHECHITA.

Arnholz, A., Esq.
Berg, Ellis, Esq.
Birnbaum, B., Esq.
Davis, David, Esq.
Goldhill, J., Esq.
Hymans, Henry, Esq.
Israel, H. A., Esq.
Levy, J., Esq.

Levy, Lewis, Esq.
Simmons, S., Esq.
London, P., Esq.
Marks, I. M., Esq.
Montagu, Samuel, Esq.
Samuel, Michael, Esq.
Solomon, Henry, Esq.

AUDITORS.

Silber, A. M., Esq.

Davidson, Louis, Esq.

HONORARY OFFICERS, BOARDS OF MANAGEMENT, AND MINISTERS OF THE CONSTITUENT SYNAGOGUES.

GREAT SYNAGOGUE.—*Wardens:* Sir Nathaniel M. De Rothschild, Bart., M.P., and Mr. Abraham Rosenfeld. *Financial Representative:* Mr. Isaiah M. Marks. *Board of Management:* Messrs. Moss Benjamin, M. Bentwitch, Jos. Davis, Henry A. Isaacs, C.C., Alex. Isaacs, Ralph Lazarus, and B. Van Staveren. *Ministers:* Rev. Marcus Hast and Rev. Moses Keizer, who is also *Secretary.*

HAMBRO' SYNAGOGUE.—*Wardens:* Messrs. Harris Jacobs and S. Jacobs. *Financial Representative:* Mr. H. A. Israel. *Board of Management:* Messrs. M. Jaffe, C. Joel, M. Levy, Mark Myers, J. Reubenson, M. Rosenberg, and B. L. Van Prangh. *Ministers:* Rev. S. M. Gollancz and Rev. E. Spero. *Secretary:* Mr. Jacob Salomons.

NEW SYNAGOGUE.—*Wardens:* Messrs. D. H. Jacobs and L. Ososki. *Financial Representative:* Mr. Lewis Levy. *Board of Management:* Messrs. R. Z. Bloomfield, George Cohen, Chas. Davis, Coleman Jonas, John Jacobs, Samuel Levy, L. H. Phillips, C.C., Alg. E. Sydney, Israel Woolf, and Saul Woolf. *Preacher:* Rev. Hermann Gollancz. *Ministers:* Rev. Ab. Barnett and Rev. Isaac Cohen, who is also *Secretary.*

CENTRAL SYNAGOGUE.—*Wardens:* Messrs. J. A. Jonas and Morris S. Oppenheim. *Financial Representative:* Mr. Joseph Benjamin. *Board of Management:* Messrs. Alfred H. Beddington, Lionel L. Cohen, Fred. Davis, Asher Isaacs, J. A. Joseph, Jacob Levy, and S. Trenner. *Ministers:* Rev. Aaron L. Green, who is also *Preacher,* and Rev. S. Lyons, who is also *Secretary.*

BAYSWATER SYNAGOGUE.—*Wardens:* Messrs. Edward A. Levy and Henry Lucas. *Financial Representative:* Mr. Isaac A. Joseph. *Board of Management:* Messrs. Marcus N. Adler, J. Bergtheil, David Benjamin, Henry H. Collins, Louis Davidson, A. Flatau, and Charles Samuel. *Preacher:* Rev. Dr. Hermann Adler. *Ministers:* Rev. Isaac Samuel and Rev. Raphael Harris, who is also *Secretary.*

BORO' SYNAGOGUE.—*Wardens:* Messrs. J. A. Cohen and H. J. Solomons. *Financial Representative:* Mr. S. Weingott. *Board of Management:* Messrs. A. J. Cohen, Mark Davis, S. L. Frankenburg, E. Grauman, H. M. Harris, Moss Harris, David L. Jacobs, M. S. Joseph, Joseph Salomons, and Saul Solomon. *Ministers:* Rev. Sol. Levy and Rev. P. Ornstien, who is also *Secretary.*

ST. JOHN'S WOOD SYNAGOGUE.—*Wardens:* Messrs. Hyman, A. Abrahams and Benn Davis. *Financial Representative:* Mr. A. Arnholz. *Board of Management:* Messrs. L. Farmer, S. Marks, E. N. Frankenstein, M. de Saxe, M. L. Auerhaan, Henry H. Collins, and S. Spyer. *Preacher, Minister, and Secretary:* Rev. B. Berliner.

EAST LONDON SYNAGOGUE.—*Wardens:* Messrs. Morris Barnett and Mark Jacobs. *Financial Representative:* Mr. Ab. Levy. *Board of Management:* Messrs. D. Barnard, Isaac Cohen, J. Kaufman, Sol. Silver, Hyman Simons, H. Wolfsbergen, and M. Wolfsbergen. *Ministers:* Rev. V. Rosenstein and Rev. H. Millem, who is also *Secretary.*

NORTH LONDON SYNAGOGUE.—*Wardens:* Messrs. E. Berg and W. Flatau. *Financial Representative:* Mr. H. Lazarus.

Board of Management : Messrs. B. Birnbaum, J. Goldhill, H. Hart, H. Lazarus, J. Lindow, L. Lion, J. Magnus, and M. Van Duren. *Ministers :* Revs. H. Wasserzug and Julius A. Goulstein, who is also *Preacher* and *Secretary.*

WEST END SYNAGOGUE. — *Wardens :* Sir Barrow H. Ellis, K.C.S.I. and Mr. James L. Hart. *Financial Representative :* Mr. Neville D. Cohen. *Board of Management :* Messrs. Maurice H. Beddington, Arthur Cohen, Q.C., M.P., Ellis A. Franklin, F. M. Halford, Martin Jaffe, A. M. Marsden, F. Mendl, Sam. Montagu, Henry Nathan, S. S. Oppenheim, S. Schloss, and Saul Solomon. *Ministers :* Rev. Simeon Singer, who is also *Preacher,* and Rev. M. Haines, who is also *Secretary.*

ק״ק כנסת ישראל

UNITED SYNAGOGUE.

LAWS *of the United Synagogue and* BYE-LAWS, *made pursuant to 33 and 34 Vic., c.* 116, *for the Government of the Constituent Synagogues, and for the Regulation and Management of their Local Matters.*

את ה׳ אלהיך תירא ואתו תעבד

" *Thou shalt fear the Lord thy God, and serve Him.*"—*Deut.* vi. 13.

** *The Paragraphs Printed in Italics, being either Extracts from Acts of Parliament or Bye-laws enacted by the Council,* are NOT SUBJECT TO REVISION *by the Boards of Management of the Constituent Synagogues.*

THE *United Synagogue* ק״ק כנסת ישראל *consists, at the date of the adoption by the Council of the following Laws and Bye-laws, of the Great, Hambro', New, Bayswater and Central Synagogues, constituted Constituent Synagogues by Sec. 1 and 2 of the Schedule to the 33 and 34 Vic., c. 116 (United Synagogue Act); of the Boro' and North London Synagogues, admitted into the Union under the provisions of Sec. 63 of the said Schedule to the said Act; and of the St. John's Wood, East London and West End Synagogues, admitted under the provisions of Sec. 64 of the said Schedule.*

B

_____SYNAGOGUE.

1. *This Congregation consists of—*

Sec. 6a, Subsect. B, Schedule to United Synagogues Act.

A. Persons (whether male or female) who shall be in occupation as tenants of seats at this Synagogue.

Sec. 6a, Subsect. A, Schedule to United Synagogues Act.

B. Persons who, at the date of the passing of the resolutions amending the Schedule to the United Synagogues Act (May 24, 1880), were Privileged Members of the United Synagogue, and were attached to this Synagogue, so long as they continue to comply with the conditions which may be required and to contribute the annual payments which may be assessed by the Council of the United Synagogue, or its Executive Committee, for the maintenance of חוקת הקהלה (the rights of a Privileged Member of the United Synagogue).

Sec. 55, Schedule to United Synagogues Act.

MEMBERS OF THE UNITED SYNAGOGUE NOT HOLDING SEATS IN A CONSTITUENT SYNAGOGUE.

Sec. 6a, Subsect. C, Schedule to the United Synagogues Act.

2. Persons (whether male or female) not in occupation as tenants of Seats at any Constituent Synagogue who shall contribute to the United Synagogue such annual sum for the right of Membership as the Executive Committee shall determine, and shall not be more than one year in arrear in payment thereof, are Members of the United Synagogue.

Sec. 6a, Subsect. C, and Sect. 53, Schedule to the United Synagogues Act.

3. Any person desirous of acquiring or retaining Membership of the United Synagogue without holding a seat in a Constituent Synagogue, shall make application in writing to the Executive Committee of the United Synagogue, who shall assess the annual amount

to be paid in each case, exclusive of 18*s. per annum* Law of Burial Society.
*Burial Rate. In the event of such Member becoming
a tenant of a seat in a Constituent Synagogue, his
seniority of membership shall date from the time of his
becoming a Member of the United Synagogue, provided
he shall have regularly paid his Assessment and Burial
Rate.*

RIGHTS OF SEATHOLDERS.

4. *A male Seatholder above the age of* 21 *years,
having occupied a seat in this Synagogue for one year
immediately preceding the date of. election, and being
not more than one year in arrear in. payment of his
account, is entitled to the following rights :—*

A. He is eligible to be elected to the office of
חתן בראשית or חתן תורה.

B. *He is entitled to vote—*

> (*a.*) *At the Biennial Election of Representa-* Sec.7, of Schedule toUnited
> *tives to the Council of the United Syna-* Synagogues Act.
> *gogue ;*
>
> (*b.*) *At the Annual Election of the Board of* Sec. 41, of Schedule to United Synagogues Act.
> *Management of this Synagogue ;*
>
> (*c.*) *At the election of Salaried Officers of this* Sec. 60, of Schedule to United Synagogues Act.
> *Synagogue ;*
>
> (*d.*) *At the election of Representatives of this* Bye-law of Council.
> *Synagogue at the London Committee of
> Deputies of the British Jews ;*

*Subject to the provisions of the United Synagogues Act
and of the Bye-laws regulating such elections.*

5. *A Male Seatholder above the age of* 21 *years,
occupying a full price seat in this Synagogue, shall, if
he has occupied a full price seat at this or any other
Constituent Synagogue for the two consecutive years
immediately preceding the date of election, and is not*

*more than one year in arrear in payment of his account,
be eligible to be elected—*

<table>
<tr><td>Sec. 7, Sub-sect. F & G, Schedule to United Synagogues Act.</td><td>(a.) A Member of the Council of the United Synagogue, to represent this Synagogue thereat, in accordance with the provisions of Sec. 7, Sub-secs. F & G of the Schedule to the United Synagogues Act.</td></tr>
<tr><td>Sec. 9, Schedule to United Synagogues Act.</td><td>(b.) A Treasurer of the United Synagogue.</td></tr>
<tr><td></td><td>(c.) An Overseer of the Poor of the United Synagogue.</td></tr>
<tr><td>Secs. 41, 41a and 16 of the Schedule to the United Synagogues Act.</td><td>(d.) A Warden, Financial Representative, or Member of the Board of Management of this Synagogue in accordance with the provisions of Secs. 41 and 41a of the Schedule to the United Synagogues Act.</td></tr>
<tr><td>Bye-law of Council.</td><td>(e.) A Representative at the London Committee of Deputies of the British Jews.</td></tr>
</table>

6. A Seatholder in this Synagogue, not being more than 12 months in arrears in payment of his account, is entitled according to seniority of membership—

(*a.*) To officiate as סגן (except on ימים טובים holidays) on the occasion of the marriage and of the בר מצוה of any of his children.

(*b.*) To be called to the reading of the Law קריאת התורה on שבת whenever he is a חיוב.

(*c.*) To recite קדיש, subject to the provisions of Bye-law 164.

(*d.*) To the attendance of one of the Readers of this Synagogue on the occasion of the marriage of any of his children or the ברית מילה of any of his sons.

RIGHTS OF בעלי בתים (PRIVILEGED MEM-BERS) NOT BEING SEATHOLDERS.

This law applies to the Great, New, and Hambro' Synagogues, only.

7. *Persons who possessed* חזקת הקהלה *(the rights of a Privileged Member) of this Synagogue at the date of the establishment of the United Synagogue (14th July, 1870), and not then being occupiers of seats therein, are, so long as they shall continue to comply with the conditions required by the Council or by the Executive Committee for the maintenance of their right of Privileged Membership, entitled to vote—At the Biennial Election of Representatives at the Council of the United Synagogue.*

Sec. 7 of Schedule to United Synagogues Act.

ORDER OF PRECEDENCE OF PRIVILEGED AND OTHER MEMBERS, AND MAINTENANCE OF MEMBERSHIP.

8. *All persons who at the date of the passing of the resolutions of May 24, 1880, amending the United Synagogues Act, were Privileged Members of the United Synagogue, shall remain Privileged Members of the United Synagogue, and shall, so far as not inconsistent with the Scheme as altered or modified by those resolutions, retain their present privileges.*

Sec. 55, Schedule to United Synagogues Act.

9. *The Members of the United Synagogue shall be entitled to precedence in the Constituent Synagogues in which they hold seats according to seniority of membership, and in calculating such seniority, the date of admission shall, as to persons who at the date of the establishment of the Scheme were Privileged Members of a Constituent Synagogue, be considered to be the date at which they shall have been made Privileged Members of such Constituent Synagogue, and*

Sec. 56, Schedule to United Synagogues Act.

the date of admission shall, as to persons who between the date of the establishment of the Scheme, and the date of the passing of the resolutions of May 24th, 1880, amending the United Synagogues Act, have been made Privileged Members of the United Synagogue, be considered to be the date at which they shall have been made such Privileged Members. The other Members of the United Synagogue shall rank after the preceding, and in calculating the seniority of such other Members, the date of admission shall be the date at which they first began to occupy seats as tenants at any Constituent Synagogue, or first made payment of an annual sum for right of membership; but so that for the purpose of retaining such seniority, there must be no interval subsequent to the date of admission in which such Member shall not either have occupied a seat at a Constituent Synagogue, or been a contributor of an annual sum for right of membership in accordance with these resolutions not more than a year in arrear in payment thereof.

See Sec. 53 of Schedule to United Synagogues Act.

10. *Any Privileged Member not holding a seat in one of the Constituent Synagogues shall, in order to retain his right of Membership, pay such annual contribution to the United Synagogue, and to the Burial Society, as the Executive Committee of the United Synagogue may determine.*

Bye-law of Council.

Such payments shall be collected by the Constituent Synagogue in which the said Privileged Member last held a seat, or if he had never been a Seatholder, by such Constituent Synagogue as the said Committee shall appoint; and all the existing rights and privileges of a Privileged Member shall be liable to be forfeited, at the discretion of the Executive Committee, on the non-payment of the said contributions.

Bye-law of Council.

11. *If any Privileged Member of the United Syna-*

7

gogue shall be reported to the Executive Committee as having forfeited his seat in a Constituent Synagogue by reason of being in arrears of his account, the Executive Committee may, in their discretion, declare the said Member to have forfeited all his rights and privileges as a Privileged Member of the United Synagogue.

12. The local rights of any Seatholder, whether Privileged or Non-Privileged Member, may, at the discretion of the Board of Management, be suspended, should the said Seatholder be more than twelve months in arrear in payment of his account.

See also Bye-law 63.

13. The order of precedence among Privileged Members and Seatholders shall be that indicated in Bye-laws 176 and 179.

GOVERNMENT.

At the New and Boro' Synagogues the number of Committeemen is TEN; *at the North London* EIGHT, *and at the West End* NINE.

14. *The government of this Synagogue in respect of matters of a local nature affecting the same specified as such in the United Synagogues Act, or determined by the Bye-laws of the Council, shall be under the management of two Wardens and* seven *Committeemen, who together shall constitute a Board of Management in accordance with Sec.* 41 *of the Schedule to the United Synagogues Act.*

Vide Sec. 14, Schedule to United Synagogues Act.

15. *The Financial Representative of each Constituent Synagogue shall be ex-officio a member of its Board of Management. He shall take rank in the Synagogue immediately after the Wardens, and shall have a seat in the Wardens' box therein.*

Bye-law of Council.

16. The Wardens and the Financial Representative

for the time being of this Synagogue shall be termed Honorary Officers thereof.

WARDENS.

Vide Sec. 43, Schedule to United Synagogues Act. 17. *The Wardens of the Synagogue shall preside therein, and shall have the general superintendence of the religious service and local business thereof, subject to the provisions of any Bye-laws in force which from time to time may be made by the Council, or by the Board of Management of this Synagogue, in accordance with Sections 52 and 66 of the Schedule to the United Synagogues Act.*

18. The Wardens shall arrange between themselves the rota of their duties, one of them acting as Warden President for the time being.

19. The Warden President shall officiate as סגן, except when such function shall devolve by right on any Seatholder under the provisions of Bye-laws 169 and 170 ; but he shall have the power of delegating such duty to either of the other two Honorary Officers.

20. Every proclamation made in the Synagogue, and every notice paper affixed therein, or in any part thereof, or on any building belonging thereto, shall require the previous consent of the Presiding Honorary Officer, or the order of the Board of Management of this Synagogue, or of the Council of the United Synagogue.

RECEIPT AND EXPENDITURE OF MONEY.
FINANCIAL REPRESENTATIVE.

Vide Sec. 16, Schedule to United Synagogues Act. 21. *The person elected by each Constituent Synagogue in accordance with the provisions of Section 16 of the Schedule to the United Synagogues Act, shall be called its Financial Representative.*

22. *The Financial Representative shall superintend* Bye-law of Council.
the receipt and expenditure of all money on account of
this Synagogue, and the receipt of money in connection Vide Sec. 15, Schedule to the
therewith on account of the Burial Society, subject as United Synagogues Act.
to both to the general superintendence of the Treasurers
of the United Synagogue.

23. The Financial Representative shall, in the event of any person, or any immediate member of such person's family, dying while in arrear of his or their account to the Synagogue, be empowered to compromise all debts, the non-payment of which would, under the Laws of the Burial Society, entail deprivation of the rights and privileges of that Society.

24. *All the moneys received on behalf of the Con-* Bye-law of Council.
stituent Synagogues shall be paid into the account of
the Bankers of the United Synagogue. Such payments
shall be made under the supervision of the Financial
Representative.

25. (*a.*) A list of cheques for the payment of the quarterly, monthly and other disbursements of this Synagogue, shall, at least one week before such cheques are required, be prepared and forwarded by the Secretary, under the direction of the Financial Representative, to the Secretary of the United Synagogue. All demand notes must be signed by the Financial Representative, and countersigned by the Secretary.

(*b.*) *Demand notes for sums of money to be ex-* Bye-law of Council.
pended under Clause 47 of the Schedule to the United
Synagogues Act, must state explicitly the object for which
such sums are required; and no sum drawn under any
item or items in the Estimates, or under the said
Clause, shall be available for granting a gratuity, com-
pensation, or increase of salary, to any official, or class
of officials.

26. *The Financial Representative of each Constituent Synagogue shall, whenever requested so to do by the Treasurers of the United Synagogue, forward to the Secretary of the United Synagogue a statement to be prepared by the Local Secretary in such form as the said Treasurers shall deem necessary or expedient, showing the financial position of such Constituent Synagogue.*

27. *The Financial Representative shall, under the direction of the Board of Management, superintend the preparation of the annual Budget and Estimates of this Synagogue.*

28. *The Financial Representative of each Constituent Synagogue may, for the current expenditure of such Synagogue during the months of January and February of every year, draw upon the Treasurers of the United Synagogue on the same scale as authorised in the Budget of the preceding year; and after the estimates for the current year shall have been adopted by the Council, all payments made by the Financial Representative in pursuance of this law shall be adjusted with reference to the definite annual expenditure sanctioned by the Council.*

29. *The form, arrangement, and grouping of the accounts issued by each Constituent Synagogue, and of all statements relating to its finances, shall be under the supervision of the Financial Representative, in accordance with the instructions relating thereto, which shall, from time to time, be issued by the Finance Committee.*

30. The Financial Representative on entering office shall receive from the Secretary an inventory in triplicate of all ספרי תורה mantles, bells, and other ornaments thereto belonging, בגדי קודש, plate, furniture,

and other movable property in the possession or under
the care of the Secretary of this Synagogue. ·

31. The Financial Representative shall sign such
inventories, retain one copy in his possession during his
tenure of office, and shall forward another copy to the
Secretary of the United Synagogue; the third copy
shall remain in the custody of the Secretary of this
Synagogue. The Financial Representative shall see
that the property· be kept in good order and condition, and in a secure place appropriated for such purpose; that all additions to such property made during
his tenure of office be duly entered by the Secretary
in the said inventories, and shall notify such additions
to the Board of Management and to the Council.

32. The Financial Representative, at the expiration of his period of office, shall return his copy of
the inventory to the Secretary, having previously
compared the same with the property scheduled
therein; if he find the same correct, he shall certify
thereon to that effect, or report to the Board of
Management as to its incorrectness. This annual
procedure shall be observed although the same
Financial Representative remain in office for a subsequent term.

33. The movable property appertaining to this
Synagogue shall at all times remain therein, unless
removed for the purpose of repair. Provided always,
that any portion of such property may be lent to the
Executive of any other Synagogue for any temporary
purpose, upon the consent in writing being obtained
of any two of the Honorary Officers of this Synagogue and of one of the Honorary Officers of the
United Synagogue.

34. The Financial Representative shall superin-

tend the receipt of מחצית השקל in the Synagogue on פורים.

35. The Financial Representative shall, at least once in three months, inspect and examine the Books and Accounts kept by the Secretary, and shall satisfy himself that such Books and Accounts are correctly kept.

36. The Accounts of the Income and Expenditure of this Synagogue shall be annually made up to the 31st of December by the Financial Representative, and shall be laid, duly audited, before the Board of Management, and, in print, before the Finance Committee of the United Synagogue as soon after such date as they may direct.

37. The Financial Representative, or, in his absence, one of the Wardens, shall examine and sign the Members' Accounts prior to their being issued.

BOARD OF MANAGEMENT— ITS FUNCTIONS AND POWERS.

38. The Board of Management shall meet at least once every three months, or oftener if necessary, to superintend and manage all matters of a local nature affecting the Synagogue.

Sec. 45, Schedule to United Synagogues Act.

39. *The Board of Management of each Constituent Synagogue shall annually prepare and submit to the Council a Budget or Scheme, showing the estimated Income and Expenditure for the ensuing year in respect of the same Constituent Synagogue; and such Budget or Scheme shall, if and so far as the same shall not be varied by the Council within two months after the same shall be submitted, and subject to such*

variations (if any) as shall within the said two months be made by the Council, be deemed to be confirmed and adopted by the Council; and the Income and Expenditure of the ensuing year, in respect of the Constituent Synagogue, shall, as closely as may be, be regulated by and with reference to the same Budget.

40. *The Board of Management of a Constituent Synagogue shall have the general supervision and control of all Salaried Officers of the United Synagogue whose duties relate specially to the said Constituent Synagogue, and shall have power, in case of a vacancy, to appoint any such Officer, whose salary shall not exceed thirty pounds a year.* Sec. 46, Schedule to United Synagogues Act.

41. *The Board of Management of a Constituent Synagogue shall have power to direct repairs in the same Synagogue to an amount not exceeding in any one year the sum of fifty pounds, and to direct an expenditure for the General Purposes of the same Constituent Synagogue to an amount not exceeding in any one year the sum of fifty pounds.* Sec. 47, Schedule to United Synagogues Act.

See also Byelaw 50.

42. The Board of Management shall fix the day and hour for election of Salaried Officers whose duties relate specially to this Synagogue, to be elected under the provisions of Sec. 60 of the Schedule to the United Synagogues Act.

43. The Board of Management of each Constituent Synagogue may impose fines upon persons who shall be elected and shall refuse or neglect to serve the office of Warden of that Synagogue; the amount of the said fines shall be from time to time determined by such Board of Management, subject to the approbation of the Council of the United Synagogue. Clause 5 Deed of Foundation and Trust.

Bye-laws of Council.

44. *As soon as possible after the Elections held in accordance with the provisions of Section 41 or Section 41a of the Schedule to the United Synagogues Act, the Board of Management shall elect as follows :—*

> *One of their number as a Member of the Committee of the Burial Society ;*
>
> *One of their number as a Member of the Building Committee of the United Synagogue.*
>
> *One of the Wardens as a Member of the Bequests and Trusts Committee.*

45. If any paid Officer of this Synagogue be guilty of misconduct or neglect of duty, the Warden President, or in his absence, one of the other Honorary Officers, according to seniority, may suspend such Officer, but must immediately thereafter convene a Meeting of the Board of Management, to be held within seven days, to take such further steps thereon as may be deemed necessary or expedient, and in the notice convening such Meeting the purpose thereof shall be stated. If the Board of Management deem it necessary to dismiss such Officer, the resolution to that effect shall be forthwith reported to the Council, who shall confirm or reject such resolution.

Sec. 50, Schedule to United Synagogues Act.

46. *The Board of Management of a Constituent Synagogue shall have such further and other powers with reference to the management of matters of a local nature affecting the same Synagogue as shall be determined by the Council of the United Synagogue.*

Sec. 51, Schedule to United Synagogues Act.

47. *The Board of Management of a Constituent Synagogue shall be subject to the Control of the Council of the United Synagogue.*

REGULATIONS for REPAIRS and WORKS,

as Amended by the Council, January 5th, 1892.

Constituent Synagogues.

1. The Presiding Honorary Officer of a Constituent Synagogue shall, subject to the provisions of Regulation 3, have power to order repairs at or in connection with that Synagogue, provided the amount of any such repairs does not at any one time exceed £5. Every authorisation for such repairs must be given in writing, be countersigned by the Local Secretary, and be forwarded to the Secretary of the United Synagogue. Subject to the provisions of Regulation 3, the amount shall then be debited to the Building Fund.

2. Where the approximate estimate at any Constituent Synagogue for any work exceeds, at any one time, the sum of £5, the previous sanction of the Local Board shall be required for its authorisation; the copy of the Estimate and of the Resolution sanctioning it shall then be transmitted to the Secretary of the United Synagogue, and, subject to the provisions of Regulation 3, the amount shall then be debited to the Building Fund.

3. If the aggregate amount of the expenditure incurred under Regulations 1 and 2 at or in connection with any Constituent Synagogue shall have amounted in any one year to a sum of £25, no further expenditure for repairs at the cost of the Building Fund shall be incurred for that Synagogue, except with the sanction of the Chairman of the Building Committee (or, in his absence, of one of the Honorary Officers of the United Synagogue in rotation of seniority), who

shall have power to ratify any outlay previously approved by the Presiding Honorary Officer or Local Board of a Constituent Synagogue (as the case may be) to an amount not exceeding £5 at any one time, and not exceeding in the aggregate a further amount of £25 in any one year for the purposes of that Synagogue.

4. No application from a Local Board of Management for repairs at a Constituent Synagogue shall be considered by the Building Committee unless such application, together with an outline description of all works which may then appear to be requisite, whereof the cost is estimated to exceed in each Synagogue the sum of £25, be made before the 1st of December in the previous year. And after having conferred with the several Boards of Management presenting such outline description on the proposals thus submitted, the Building Committee shall report to the Council not later than the month of April in each year the works which they recommend to be undertaken in the various Synagogues during the then current year, having due regard to the necessities of each Synagogue, and to the available resources of the Building Fund. Approximate Estimates of the cost of all works recommended by the Building Committee shall at the same time be submitted to the Council.

5. No new Seats shall be erected in any part of a Constituent Synagogue without the previous consent of the Building Committee, who shall recommend to the Council from what fund the cost of erecting such Seats shall be defrayed.

6. No account shall be considered as chargeable to the Building Fund unless the proceedings in connection with the order for Works or Repairs be effected strictly in accordance with the foregoing Regulations.

7. Repairs at the BETH HAMIDRASH shall, as hitherto,
be charged to the Beth Hamidrash Account.
Should its funds not be able to meet any
required expenditure, a report thereon shall be
submitted by its Board of Management and the
Building Committee conjointly to the Council.

8. The Chairman of the Building Committee, or in his
absence one of the Honorary Officers of the United
Synagogue, in rotation of seniority, may order
any repairs or works at or in connection with
the Almshouses, or any of the Buildings belonging
to the United Synagogue, unconnected with
any particular Constituent Synagogue, and unconnected with the Cemetery Buildings and
Cemeteries, both those in use and those disused,
not exceeding £10 at any one time, or not exceeding in the aggregate £50 in any one year,
and the same shall be debited to the Building
Fund. Should the amount required exceed £10
at any one time or £50 in the aggregate in the
year, but not exceed £25 at one time or £50 in
any one year, the estimate for such works shall
be submitted to the Building Committee, and
subject to their approval, be debited to the
Building Fund. Should the amount required
exceed £50, a report thereon shall be submitted
by the Building Committee to the Council for
their approval.

9. One of the Treasurers of the Burial Society, or in
their absence, one of the Honorary Officers of the
United Synagogue, in rotation of seniority, may
order any repairs or works at or in connection with
the Cemeteries or Cemetery Buildings belonging
to the United Synagogue, both those in use and
those disused, not exceeding £10 at any one time,
or not exceeding in the aggregate £50 in any one

year, and the same shall be debited to the funds of the Burial Society. Should the amount required exceed £10 at any one time or £50 in the aggregate in the year, but not exceed £25 at one time or £50 in any one year, the estimate for such works shall be submitted to the Burial Committee, and, subject to their approval, be debited to the funds of the Burial Society. Should the amount required exceed £50, a report thereon shall be submitted by them to the Council for their approval, the works to be carried out under the supervision of the Burial Committee.

NATURE OF REPAIRS.

10. Works of a decorative character cannot be considered as chargeable to the Building Fund without the express authorisation of the Council.

BYE LAW 50. The Building Committee of the United Synagogue is charged with the maintenance of the buildings of the several Constituent Synagogues, and generally with the supervision and management of the buildings and lands belonging to the United Synagogue, other than the Cemeteries or Cemetery Buildings, both those in use and those disused, for which the Burial Committee shall be responsible, as provided for in No. 9 of the Building Regulations.

LAW 19 OF THE BURIAL SOCIETY. That the Burial Committee shall inspect periodically the Burial Grounds of the Congregation (including those disused) and the Buildings thereon, and report to the General Council all repairs and alterations necessary to be made therein, such repairs and alterations to be effected in accordance with the provisions of No. 9 of the Building Regulations; and shall direct and superintend the salaried Officers of this [Burial] Society in the performance of their duties.

AUDITORS.

48.   The Board of Management shall annually appoint two Seatholders of this Synagogue to audit its Accounts.

49.   The Auditors shall at least once in six months inspect the books and receipts of this Synagogue, investigate its accounts, and certify as to their correctness.   They shall audit the annual balance-sheet of the Income and Expenditure of the Synagogue up to the 31st December in each year, as prepared under the direction of the Financial Representative, and sign it, when found correct.   Such balance-sheet shall be submitted, together with the annual budget, to the Board of Management prior to its presentation to the Finance Committee of the United Synagogue.

BUILDING COMMITTEE OF THE UNITED SYNAGOGUE.

50.   *The Building Committee of the United Syna-* Bye-law of *gogue is charged with the maintenance of the build-* Council. *ings of the several Constituent Synagogues, and of the Cemeteries, and generally with the supervision and management of the buildings and lands belonging to the United Synagogue.*

51.   *The Board of Management of a Constituent* Sec. 47, *Synagogue may* [*in accordance with Bye-law* 41] United Syna- *originate and carry out repairs and other works at* gogues Act. *their own Synagogue at a cost not exceeding £50 in* Bye-law of *any one year; but when the approximate estimate* Council. *of such repairs or works exceeds the sum of £50, the*

Board of Management shall invite the assistance of the Building Committee thereon; and their joint report shall be presented to the Council of the United Synagogue, and shall be accompanied by an estimate of the cost of the repairs and other works. And it shall be the duty of the Building Committee to report to the Council as to whether any proportion, and if any, what proportion of the estimated cost should (having due regard to the special circumstances of each case) be considered as chargeable to the general account of the United Synagogue.

Bye-law of Council.

52. *All questions affecting the light, air, or other easements of any Constituent Synagogue, or appurtenances thereof, or of any other United Synagogue property, or affecting the value or rights of such property directly, indirectly, or in reversion, and all questions involving structural alterations to such properties, shall be deemed matters beyond the control of any Committee other than the Building Committee of the United Synagogue; and any such question shall be accordingly not dealt with by any Local Board of Management, but shall be forthwith, directly it shall have cognizance of such question, referred by it to the Building Committee; and it shall be the duty of the Surveyor appointed by the Council to report to and advise the Building Committee upon all such questions. Nothing in this Bye-law shall be held to affect the choice of an Architect for the erection or re-building of a Constituent Synagogue.*

SEATS.

Sec. 48, Schedule to United Synagogue Act.

53. *The Board of Management of a Constituent Synagogue shall fix the rentals to be paid for the*

(55b.) "If, in contravention of the conditions mentioned in Bye-Laws relating to members in arrears, any Constituent Synagogue shall accept as a member any person indebted to another Constituent Synagogue, the offending Synagogue shall pay to such other Constituent Synagogue all sums received from such defaulting member, until the whole of the arrears shall be liquidated, and that the provisions of this Bye-Law be retrospective so far as members accepted during 1899."

No salaried officer shall be permitted to canvass either the members of the Council, or any Committee thereof, in respect of any application for increase of salary or grant from the funds administered by the United

use of seats thereat, and submit the same to the Council, and such rentals shall, if and so far as the same shall not be varied by the Council within two months after the same shall be submitted, and subject to such variations, if any, as shall within the said two months be made by the Council, be deemed to be confirmed and adopted by the Council, and take effect from and after the expiration of the said two months, until the same shall be varied by the said Board of Management and Council in manner aforesaid.

54. The Honorary Officers shall supervise and direct the letting of the seats in the Synagogue in accordance with the charges for the same fixed by the Board of Management of this Synagogue, and approved of by the Council of the United Synagogue.

55. No person shall be permitted to rent a seat in this Synagogue while he shall be indebted to any other Constituent Synagogue of the United Synagogue, unless by the written permission of the Honorary Officers of the Synagogue to which he is indebted.

56. *Seats may be let, at the discretion of the Board of Management of a Constituent Synagogue, to the unmarried sons of a Member, at half the fixed rentals, subject to the regulations contained in Bye-laws 57, 58, 59, 60 and 61.* Bye-law of Council.

57. *Every application for a seat at half-price in a Constituent Synagogue shall be submitted to its Board of Management, a specific resolution of which Board shall be necessary for the granting of such application.* Bye-law of Council.

58. *At the close of, in each case, every three years' occupation, the Board of Management of a Constituent Synagogue shall take into consideration the tenancy of* Bye-law of Council.

c

Bye-law of
Council
every Seatholder at half-price in such Synagogue, and shall determine whether it shall be continued.

59. *If a person has held a seat in a Synagogue at half-price while under 25 years of age, and on attaining that age desires to continue the occupancy at that price, he shall make application to the Board of Management, who shall have power to adjudicate thereon.*

60. *The privilege of holding seats at a reduced rate can only be retained while the parents of the occupant, or one of them, holds a seat or seats in one of the Constituent Synagogues, unless the Board of Management of the Synagogue in which such seat is held at a reduced price shall resolve to the contrary in each particular case, on an application being made to it by such Seatholder.*

Bye-law of
Council.
Bye-law of
Council.
61. *The Board of Management of each Constituent Synagogue shall determine if any and what limit shall be placed upon the number of seats at half-price which may be allowed to the family of any one Member; and shall, at the commencement of each financial year, report to the Executive Committee of the United Synagogue the number of seats in such Constituent Synagogue let at half-price.*

62. The Board of Management may grant the use of a free seat or seats in this Synagogue, for a term not exceeding one year; and in the event of its exercising this power, shall, at the commencement of each financial year, report to the Executive Committee of the United Synagogue the number of seats so granted.

See also Bye-
laws 11 and
12.
63. If a Seatholder in this Synagogue (being more than twelve months in arrear in his payments to the Synagogue) neglect or refuse to pay his

Addition to Bye-Law 63 -

"The foregoing Bye-law shall apply only to Seatholders
who have been contributing members and not in arrear
of their Accounts for two consecutive years. Should
a Seatholder of less than two years' standing be in
arrear for more than half-a-year, his seat shall be
liable to forfeiture at the discretion of the Board of
Management, upon the expiration of one month's notice
forwarded to such member, demanding payment of his a/c
and signifying that his seat will be liable to forfeiture.

account after the delivery thereof, a notice demanding payment of such arrears within three calendar months thereafter, shall be delivered at his last known place of residence; and in the event of such Seatholder neglecting to make payment pursuant to such demand, a second notice shall be delivered, as aforesaid; and if within three months from the service of such second notice the amount due by such Seatholder be not paid, his seat at the Synagogue shall be liable to forfeiture at the discretion of the Board of Management, but such forfeiture shall not relieve the defaulting party from the payment of such account; nevertheless, it shall be in the power of the Honorary Officers to compromise the debt due by any Seatholder, and to accept payment on account from him.

64. *Should any Privileged Member of the United Synagogue be declared by the Board of Management to have forfeited his seat under the provisions of the foregoing Bye-Law, the fact of such forfeiture shall be immediately reported to the Executive Committee of the United Synagogue.* Bye-law of Council.

65. *The accounts for seat rentals and taxation shall be issued half-yearly, in the months of Nissan and Ellul, and shall be charged in advance. In the case of existing Seatholders to whom accounts have not been hitherto rendered in this manner, this Bye-Law shall not be imposed.* Bye-law of Council.

BEQUESTS.

66. The name of every testator bequeathing the sum of £10 or upwards to the funds of the United Synagogue, and the name of every person in whose memory a donation of £10 or upwards is given, shall be

c 2

inscribed on tablets appropriated for the purpose on the premises of that Constituent Synagogue in which such deceased person was a Seatholder, or such other Constituent Synagogue as the testator or donor shall select, in such manner and place as the Board of Management of such Synagogue shall direct; and if the testator was not, or the donor is not a Seatholder of any Constituent Synagogue, then the gift or donation shall be recorded in such manner and place as the Council may direct; unless such testator or his executors or such donor, as the case may be, shall request that such inscription be not made.

MEETINGS.

67. All Meetings of the Board of Management shall be convoked by order of the Warden President, for such days and such hours as he shall think fit; subject always to the provisions of Bye Law No. 38.

68. A summons containing a notice of the time appointed for holding a Meeting of the Board of Management, and setting forth, as far as possible, the matters for consideration thereat, shall be forwarded by the Secretary to every Member of such Board at least seven days prior to each Meeting, unless the urgency of the business shall not admit of such summons being so forwarded, when such notice as time will permit shall be given.

69. Should the Annual Budgets or Estimates propose any extraordinary or special outlay, or any addition to the existing expenditure, or to the salary of any officer, exceeding £20 in any one item, or should such outlay or addition be proposed during the year, the said outlay, salary or addition, shall be

inserted in the agenda of the summons convening the Meeting which is to consider the same, and shall be specifically voted upon.

70. *One of the Wardens of a Constituent Syna-* Sec. 42, Schedule to *gogue shall preside at all Meetings of the Board of* the United *Management thereof at which they or one of them* Synagogues Act. *shall be present. If both of the Wardens shall be absent from a Meeting, the Members present shall elect one of their number to be Chairman.*

71. *All acts, matters, and questions to be done,* Sec. 44, Schedule to *determined, and decided by the Board of Management* the United *of a Constituent Synagogue, shall be done, determined,* Synagogues Act. *and decided by the majority of persons present at a Meeting of the said Board. The Chairman at any of such Meetings shall, in case of equality of votes, have* At North Lon- *a double or casting vote. Three persons* don Synagogue FIVE form a *shall, until otherwise determined by the* quorum. *said Board, form a quorum at any Meeting thereof.*

72. The Secretary shall attend every Meeting of the Board of Management, take down the minutes of its proceedings in a book, and afterwards transcribe the same into the minute book of the Board of Management, from which book the minutes shall be read at the next ensuing Meeting of such Board.

73. At every Meeting of the Board of Management the minutes of the preceding Meeting shall be read by the Secretary, and if they have been correctly recorded, shall be confirmed. Upon the motion to confirm such minutes being put from the chair no discussion shall be allowed thereon, except as to their correctness.

74. Any three Members of the Board of Manage-

mont, or any fifteen Seatholders of this Synagogue, (such Scatholders not being more than twelve months in arrear in payment of their accounts to the Synagogue), may, by requisition in writing, stating therein the subject to be considered, require the Warden President to convene a Meeting of the Board of Management for that special purpose, and such Meeting shall be convoked by the Warden President within three clear days from the receipt of such requisition, to be held at a period not later than seven days thereafter.

75. One-eighth of the total number of male Seatholders of this Synagogue (such Seatholders not being more than twelve months in arrear in payment of their accounts to this Synagogue) may, by requisition in writing, stating therein the subject to be considered, require the Warden President to convene a Meeting of the Seatholders of this Synagogue for that special purpose, and such meeting shall be convoked by the Warden President within seven days from the receipt of such requisition, to be held within seven days thereafter. At such Meeting thirty shall form a quorum, and the order of proceedings thereat shall, as far as practicable, be regulated in conformity with the provisions applicable to Meetings of the Board of Management under Sections 42 and 44 of the Schedule to the United Synagogues Act.

At the Boro' Synagogue this power is given to ONE-TENTH of the Seatholders.

At the Boro', North London, and West End Synagogues, TWENTY to be a quorum; at St. John's Wood, ONE-FOURTH of the male Seatholders to form a quorum.

76. All General Meetings of the Congregation of this Synagogue, for whatever purpose the same shall be held, shall be convoked by notice issued to each Member of the Congregation entitled to attend thereat

not less than seven days prior to the date of the Meeting; and the summons issued for convoking the Meeting shall set forth, as far as possible, the matters for consideration thereat.

77. At every Meeting the Presiding Honorary Officer shall take the chair.

78. The decision of the majority at every Meeting shall be binding on the minority.

79. The Chairman of every Meeting shall, in case of equality of votes, have a double or casting vote.

80. The voting shall be by show of hands, unless the Chairman shall deem it expedient to have the voting taken by ballot.

At the Boro', North London, and West End Synagogues, TWENTY to be a quorum; at St. John's Wood, ONE-FOURTH of the male Seat-holders to form a quorum.

81. The persons present at a General Meeting duly convened shall be considered as representing the whole of the Congregation, provided that not less than thirty persons entitled to vote be present. See Bye-law 75.

82. The Warden President of a Constituent Synagogue shall summon a Meeting of the Board of Management, or a General Meeting of the Seatholders of such Synagogue, if and when required to do so by the Council, and for such purpose as the Council may direct. Bye-law of Council.

83. In the event of the Warden President failing to convoke either a regular or special Meeting of the Board of Management, or any Meeting duly demanded by requisition, or ordered by the Council, the duty of convoking such Meeting shall devolve on the other Warden, and upon his failing to do so, on the Financial Representative. Should, however, any such

Meeting not be convoked by any of the aforesaid Honorary Officers, it shall be in the power of any three Members of the Board of Management to direct the Secretary, by notification in writing signed by them, to summon such Meeting.

ELECTION OF REPRESENTATIVES OF THE CONSTITUENT SYNAGOGUE AT THE COUNCIL OF THE UNITED SYNAGOGUE, AND OF MEMBERS OF THE BOARD OF MANAGEMENT.

Sec.7,Schedule to the United Synagogues Act.

84. *The Council of the United Synagogue shall consist of the following persons :—*

(A.) *The two Wardens for the time being of each of the Constituent Synagogues.*

(B.) *The two Treasurers for the time being of the United Synagogue.*

(C.) *The two Overseers for the time being of the Poor of the United Synagogue.*

(D.) *The two Treasurers for the time being of the Burial Society of the United Synagogue.*

(E.) *All persons who shall have served, or paid a fine for refusal to serve, any of the offices following, that is to say, President of the United Synagogue, Vice-President of the United Synagogue, Treasurer of the United Synagogue, and Overseer of the Poor of the United Synagogue.*

(F.) *Male persons of the age of twenty-one years and upwards, not being at the time of election members of any of the preceding classes, who shall during the whole of two consecutive years immediately pre-*

ceding the date of election have occupied seats as full price tenants at any of the Constituent Synagogues (that is to say, either during the whole of such period at one, or during part at one and the remainder at another or others of the Constituent Synagogues), and shall not at the date of election have been more than a year in arrear in payment of their accounts to the United Synagogue, to be elected by the Constituent Synagogues, in manner following, that is to say : There shall in the year 1881, and in every alternate year thereafter, be held a meeting at each of the Constituent Synagogues, and at such meeting there shall be elected one person (being at the time of election a full price Seatholder of such Synagogue) for every whole number of fifty seats in the part of the same Synagogue appropriated to men, which three months before the date of the meeting were in the occupation of tenants, and which have before the date of the summoning of the meeting been duly returned to the Council of the United Synagogue as in such occupation. The persons entitled to vote at the meeting shall be all male persons of the age of twenty-one years and upwards, who shall during the whole of the year immediately preceding the date thereof have occupied seats at the same Constituent Synagogue as tenants, and shall not, at the date of the meeting, have been more than a year in arrear in payment of their accounts to the United Synagogue, and also all Privileged Members of the United Syna-

gogue, who at the date of the establishment of the scheme were *Privileged Members* of one of the Synagogues following, that is to say, the *Great, Hambro', and New Synagogue,* and shall not have been in such occupation as aforesaid of seats in the said Constituent Synagogue, provided that such *Privileged Members* shall vote only at that *Constituent Synagogue* of which they were *Privileged Members* at the date of the establishment of the scheme, and shall not at the date of the meeting have been more than a year in arrear in payment of their accounts to the *United Synagogue,* and that they shall not in the same year have voted at a like meeting at another Constituent Synagogue. *For the purposes of this section,* the occupation, previously to admission, of seats as tenants at a Synagogue which shall be admitted as a *Constituent Synagogue* within the prescribed period of *two years or one year (as the case may be)* shall be equivalent to occupation of seats as tenants at the same Synagogue as or in the character of a Constituent Synagogue; and accounts which at the date of the admission of a Synagogue shall be due or accruing due to it from any person, shall, in determining whether or how long such person shall have been in arrear in payment of his accounts to the *United Synagogue,* be considered as forming part of such *last-mentioned accounts.* The present elected Members of the Council shall serve until the time in the year 1881 at *which the persons to be elected thereat shall commence to serve.*

(G.) Male persons of the age of twenty-one years and upwards, not being at the time of election members of any of the preceding classes, who shall during the whole of the two consecutive years immediately preceding the date of election have occupied seats as full price tenants at any of the Constituent Synagogues (that is to say, either during the whole of such period at one, or during part at one and the remainder at another or others of the Constituent Synagogues), and shall not at the date of election have been more than a year in arrear in payment of their accounts to the United Synagogue, to be elected, forthwith after its admission by a Synagogue which shall after the date of the passing of these resolutions be admitted as a Constituent Synagogue, in manner following that is to say: There shall forthwith after the admission of such Synagogue, be held a meeting at the said Synagogue, and at such meeting there shall be elected one person (being at the time of election a full price Seatholder of such Synagogue), for every whole number of fifty Seats in the part of the same Synagogue appropriated to men, which at the date of its admission as a Constituent Synagogue, were in the occupation of tenants, and which have before the date of the summoning of the said meeting been duly returned to the Council of the United Synagogue as in such occu-

pation. The persons entitled to vote at the meeting, shall be all male persons of the age of twenty-one years and upwards, who, in the case of a Synagogue admitted under the clause hereby substituted for Clause 63 of the Scheme, shall during the whole of the year immediately preceding the date of the meeting have occupied seats as tenants at the same Synagogue (whether previously or subsequently to its admission), and in the case of a Synagogue admitted under the clause hereby substituted for Clause 64 of the Scheme, shall during the whole of the year immediately preceding the date of the meeting as tenants at any of the Constituent Synagogues (that is to say, either during the whole at one, or during part at one and the remainder at another or others of the Constituent Synagogues) and in each case shall not at the date of the meeting have been more than a year in arrear in payment of their accounts to the United Synagogue. For the purposes of this section, the occupation, previously to admission, of seats as tenants at a Synagogue which shall be admitted as a Constituent Synagogue, within the prescribed period of two years or one year (as the case may be), shall be equivalent to occupation of seats as tenants at the same Synagogue as or in the character of a Constituent Synagogue, and accounts which at the date of admission of a Synagogue shall be due or accruing due to it from any person, shall in determining whether or how long such person shall have been in arrear in payment of his accounts to the United Synagogue, be considered as forming part of such last-mentioned accounts. The persons elected at an Election held at a Constituent Synagogue under this section, shall serve until the time in the year of their Election at which the persons elected at the next following Election, held at the same Constituent Synagogue under the last preceding section, shall commence to serve.

85. *Each of the Constituent Synagogues shall, in* Sec. 41, Schedule to the United Synagogues Act. *respect of such matters of a local nature affecting the same Synagogue as are specified in the Scheme and as have been or shall be hereafter determined by the Council of the United Synagogue, be under the immediate management of a body, which shall be called the Board of Management of the said Constituent Synagogue, and shall consist of the two Wardens for the time being of the Constituent Synagogue, and of not less than five other persons, who shall be called* See Bye-law 14. *Committeemen. The said Wardens and Committeemen shall be male persons of the age of twenty-one years and upwards at the time of election, in the occupation as full-priced tenants of seats at the said Constituent Synagogue, who shall during the whole of two consecutive years immediately preceding the date of election have occupied seats as full-price tenants at any of the Constituent Synagogues (that is to say, either during the whole at one, or during part at one and the remainder at another or others of the Constituent Synagogues), and shall not at the date of election have been more than a year in arrear in payment of their accounts to the United Syna-*

gogue; and they shall be elected in manner following, that is to say :—There shall in the year 1881, and in every year thereafter, be held a meeting at such Constituent Synagogue for the election of such Wardens and Committeemen; the persons entitled to vote at the meeting shall be all male persons of the age of twenty-one years and upwards who shall during the whole of the year immediately preceding the date thereof, have been in occupation of seats at the same Constituent Synagogue as tenants and shall not at the date of such election have been more than a year in arrear in payment of their accounts to the United Synagogue. For the purposes of this clause, the occupation, previously to admission, of seats as tenants at a Synagogue which shall be admitted as a Constituent Synagogue, within the prescribed period of two years or one year (as the ·case may be), shall be equivalent to occupation of seats as Tenants at the same Synagogue as or in the character of a Constituent Synagogue, and accounts which at the date of the admission of a Synagogue shall be due or accruing due to it from any person, shall in determining whether or how long such person shall have been in arrear in payment of his accounts to the United Synagogue, be considered as forming part of such last-mentioned accounts. The present Wardens and Committeemen of each of the Constituent Synagogues shall hold office and serve until the time in the year 1881 at which the Wardens and Persons to be elected at the same Synagogue under this clause shall commence to hold office and serve; and the Persons to be elected under this clause shall hold office and be Members of the Board of Management from such time in the year of their Election as the Council of the United Synagogue shall determine, until in the year of the next like Election their successors shall commence to hold office and become Members of·the

Board. *In case of either of the Wardens of a Constituent Synagogue dying, resigning or becoming incapable to act during his term of office, a successor* See Bye-law No. 106. *may thereupon be elected in like manner, and shall hold office during the remainder of the said term.*

86. *In case a Representative for the time being of a Constituent Synagogue at the Council becomes en-* Bye-law of Council. *titled to a seat at the Council by virtue of some other tenure, or resigns, or becomes incapable to act, or dies, during his term of office, a successor may thereupon be* See Bye-law No. 106. *elected in the manner provided for the Election of Representatives at the Council, and shall hold office during the remainder of the said term.*

87. *The meeting for the Annual and Biennial* Bye-law of Council. *Election, provided for in Sections 7 and 41 of the Schedule to the United Synagogues Act, shall be held in the months of* ניסן *or* אייר, *on. such day as shall be determined by the Council.*

88. *The elections shall be held at such hour as shall* Bye-law of Council. *be determined by the Warden President, or Board of Management of each Constituent Synagogue, and shall be conducted by the Presiding Officer of such Synagogue. The poll shall be kept open for a period of at least two hours.*

89. *The Biennial Election at the Constituent* Bye-law of Council. *Synagogues shall be for Representatives at the General Council of the United Synagogue; the number of such Representatives being in accordance with the provisions of Sec. 7, Sub.-sec. F. of the Schedule to the United Synagogues Act.*

90. *The Annual Election at each Constituent* Bye-law of Council. *Synagogue shall be for two Wardens, and for such number of Committeemen as are required to be*

elected under Bye-law 14, who, together with the Financial Representative, shall constitute its Board of Management.

Bye-law of Council.

91. *Immediately after the declaration by the Presiding Officer of the return of persons elected as Representatives at the Council, it shall be competent to any two persons qualified to vote, to propose from among the persons so elected, a person to fill the office of Financial Representative; and the Presiding Officer shall take a show of hands with regard to the person or persons so proposed, and shall declare the person receiving the largest number of votes to be the person duly elected as Financial Representative, unless, previously to such show of hands, not less than seven persons qualified to vote at such meeting, do, by request in writing, demand a ballot, which shall then be forthwith taken, and the result of such ballot immediately declared. No names shall be submitted to the meeting for election after such show of hands or ballot shall have been ordered to be taken. The provisions of Bye-Laws 99, 100, 101, 102, 103, 104, 105 shall apply to elections under this Bye-Law.*

Bye-law of Council.

92. *Every Elector may nominate for any of the offices of Representative at the Council, Warden, and Member of the Board of Management, any qualified person or persons, not exceeding the number of vacancies to be filled up. Such nomination shall be on a form provided, which shall be forwarded by the Local Secretary to every Elector at least twenty-one days prior to the day of election, and a period of not less than seven days from the receipt of such form shall be allowed for filling up and returning the same to the office of the Constituent Synagogue. A list of the Members duly qualified for election to the above offices shall be forwarded with every nomination paper.*

Bye-law of Council.

93. *All nominations received after the day fixed for the return of the nomination forms, and all nomination forms containing a greater number of names than there are respectively offices to fill, shall be invalid.*

Bye-law of Council.

94. *Immediately after the receipt by the Secretary of the nomination forms, he shall communicate with every nominee, informing him of the office*

for which he has been nominated; every nominee shall be entitled to decline being placed upon the nomination list, but should the Secretary receive no reply to his communication within two clear days, it shall be assumed that the nominee permits himself to be put in nomination, and his name shall appear in the nomination list to be prepared by the Secretary.

95. The Secretary shall, at least ten days prior to the election, and subject to the provisions of the preceding Bye-law, prepare a nomination list of all Members nominated for offices from the nomination forms which shall have been forwarded to him, and the election shall be made from the persons whose names are on such list; and no Member shall be eligible for election unless his name appear on such nomination list. Bye-law of Council.

96. The names of the gentlemen whose term of office is about to expire, shall be printed in the nomination list under the headings of their respective offices, and shall be distinguished by a star. They shall be previously communicated with in the manner prescribed by and subject to the provisions of Bye-law 93. Bye-law of Council.

97. At least eight days prior to the election a list of all Members who shall have been nominated for the vacant offices, in accordance with the preceding Bye-laws, shall be forwarded to every Elector by the Secretary of the Constituent Synagogue. Bye-law of Council.

98. The voting shall be by ballot; every Elector, on his presenting himself for voting, shall be furnished by the Presiding Officer with a paper containing a list of the persons nominated for the various offices for which the election is being held, on the margin of which paper the voter shall mark off the Bye-law of Council.

D

names of the persons for whom he votes. Each voting paper shall, before it is issued by the Presiding Officer, be stamped with the name of the Synagogue at which the Election is held, and any paper received without being so stamped, or which contains a greater number of votes than there are vacancies to be filled, shall be void. The voting paper shall be handed by the voter to the Presiding Officer, who shall immediately deposit it in the ballot-box.

Bye-law of Council.

See Bye-laws 4 and 56.

99. *At Elections or Meetings, no person under the age of twenty-one shall be entitled to vote. .Persons holding seats at half-price in their own names, being above the age of twenty-one years, and not more than a year in arrear in payment of their accounts to the United Synagogue, shall be entitled to vote.*

Bye-law of Council.

100. *The candidates having the largest number of votes shall be deemed elected ; but no person shall be deemed elected if he shall have received less than seven votes.*

Bye-law of Council.

101. *In case any person elected shall refuse to serve the office to which he has been elected, or by virtue of some other tenure shall be entitled to a seat at the Council or Board of Management, the person having the next largest number of votes shall be deemed duly elected, provided he shall have received not fewer than seven votes.*

Bye-law of Council.

102. *When an equality of votes between any of the candidates is found to exist at an election, the Presiding Officer shall give the casting vote immediately on the result of the election being announced.*

Bye-law of Council.

103. *No person shall be eligible for election as a Warden or Committeeman of a Constituent Synagogue, or as a Representative of such Synagogue at*

104*a*. *The result of every election to any office,* Bye-law of Council. *honorary or salaried, or of Representatives at the Council of the United Synagogue, or of Members of the Board of Management of a Constituent Synagogue shall be forthwith notified to the Central Office by the Secretary of the Constituent Synagogue holding the election; and the said return of the result shall be accompanied by a declaration by such Secretary that the person elected was eligible according to the scheme scheduled to the United Synagogues Act and the Bye Laws of the United Synagogue, so far as the same respectively apply to the particular case, and that all the requirements prescribed by the said scheme and Bye Laws, so far as the same respectively apply in connection with such election, have been complied with.*

the Council of the United Synagogue, if he be more than twelve months in arrear of payment of his account due to a Constituent Synagogue.

104. At every meeting for election, not more than three persons entitled to vote at such election, and whose names are not in the nomination list, shall be appointed by the Electors present from amongst themselves to act as scrutineers, who shall open the ballot-boxes and ascertain the result of the poll by counting the votes given to each candidate, and shall make out a list of the number of votes recorded for each of the same, and deliver such list to the Presiding Officer, who shall forthwith declare to be elected those Members to whom the majority of votes shall have been given. *Bye-law of Council.*

105. No Salaried Officer of the United Synagogue or of a Constituent Synagogue, shall be eligible for election as a Member of the Board of Management or as a Representative to the Council; and any Member of such Board, or Council, accepting any such salaried office shall thereby become ineligible to continue a Member of the same during the receipt of such salary. Any Member of the Board of Management, or of the Council, receiving a charitable allowance from the funds of the United Synagogue shall thereby become disqualified to sit at such Board during the period of his receiving such allowance. *Bye-law of Council.*

106. The power of determining the necessity for the election of a successor in case of vacancy in the offices of Warden or Representative at the Council shall vest in the Board of Management. *Vide Sections 27 and 41, Schedule to the United Synagogues Act. See Bye-laws 85 and 86.*

ELECTION OF LOCAL OFFICERS.

107. Whenever a vacancy shall occur in any office, the duties of which relate specially to a Constituent *Sec. 60, Schedule to the United*

Synagogues Act.

Synagogue, and the salary of which shall be greater than £30 a year, the Board of Management of the said Constituent Synagogue shall give public notice of the existence of the vacancy, and such notice shall state the nature of the vacant office, the salary thereof, and the qualifications necessary therefor, and shall appoint a time for receiving applications from persons desiring to be candidates for the said office; and the Board shall approve from among such persons of a person or persons as a candidate or candidates for the said office; and a Meeting shall be held for the election of a person, being the approved candidate, or one of the approved candidates, to fill the said office; and the persons entitled to vote at the said Meeting shall be all male persons who shall during the whole of the year immediately preceding the date thereof have been in occupation of seats at the said Constituent Synagogue as tenants, and shall not at the date of such Meeting have been more than a year in arrear in payment of their accounts to the United Synagogue, and also all Privileged Members not holding seats, and all widows of Privileged Members of the Synagogues following, that is to say, the Great, Hambro', and New Synagogues, who at the date of the establishment of this scheme are entitled to vote at one of the same Synagogues, shall continue to have the right

See Clause 53 of Schedule to United Synagogues Act.

of voting at that Synagogue, so long as they shall continue to comply with the conditions required by the Council for the maintenance of their rights of Privileged Membership.

See Sect. 58 of Schedule to United Synagogues Act.

108. *The power of determining the nature of the duties to be required from the Local Salaried Officers of the Constituent Synagogues, and the amount of salary to be paid to them shall rest with the Council of the United Synagogue, which determination shall be come to after receiving from the Board of*

Management of the Synagogue in which such office is vacant, a Report upon the duties of the office, and the proposed salary.

PREACHER.—READERS חזנים.

109. A Preacher may be appointed subject to Bye-law 161, and shall, if required by the Board of Management, deliver a sermon on Sabbaths and on such Holydays as may be determined by the Wardens, and on any special occasions when requested by the Wardens or the Committee.

110. The Preacher shall also, if requested, deliver a discourse at least once at the house of mourning of any Seatholder of this Synagogue during the week of mourning.

111. The Preacher and חזנים (Readers) shall, upon their election, become ex-officio נאמנים (accredited Officers) of the Congregation.

112. The חזנים (Readers), dressed in their official costume, shall attend in the Synagogue whenever Divine Service is to be performed therein, and shall enter the Synagogue for that purpose at least five minutes prior to the time fixed for the commencement of prayers.

113. The official costume of the Readers shall be such as is approved by the Board of Management.

114. The order and rotation in which the חזנים shall perform Divine Service in the Synagogue shall from time to time be regulated by the Board of Management.

115. The Readers, unless prevented by illness, shall not absent themselves from the performance of their duties in the Synagogue without the permission of the Warden President. Should either of them be unable through illness or other cause to attend the Synagogue to officiate therein, he shall intimate such inability to his colleague, who shall officiate in his stead.

Vide Bye-laws 134 & 135. 116. The Readers, in their official costume, shall attend at the solemnisation of all Marriages requiring registration or record by the Secretary of this Synagogue, whether the ceremony be performed in the Synagogue or its premises, or elsewhere; one of the Readers shall also attend, if required, at the festivals of Marriages solemnised in connection with this Synagogue, to read the customary prayers; priority, in the event of more than one Marriage being celebrated on the same day, being given to בעלי בתים and Seat-holders according to their respective seniority.

117. One of the Readers, in such rotation as may be regulated by the Honorary Officers, shall, if required, attend the ברית מילה of the son of a בעל בית, or of a Seatholder, according to seniority; and shall also attend at the Synagogue on the occasion of the wife of any Seatholder returning thanks there after childbirth.

The Great, New, and East London Synagogues do not adopt the latter portion of this clause; the Central Synagogue adds in the latter portion that the Readers shall attend "in Official Costume."

Law of Burial Society. 118. *In the case of the death of a Seatholder of a Constituent Synagogue, or of his wife, it shall be the duty of one of the Readers of such Synagogue to attend at the house of mourning on the occasion of the funeral; but when the interment takes place in the West Ham Cemetery, the Reader shall not be required to attend the funeral to the grave, unless when officiating for the Rabbi of the Burial Ground.*

Attendance on Funerals at the Cemeteries shall be regulated as follows :—

(a.) *At West Ham the duty shall devolve on the Kabronim Rabbi.*

(b.) *At Willesden it shall devolve on one of the Readers of the Synagogue to which the deceased was attached, and in the case of non-members, upon the Chief Reader of the Bayswater Synagogue.*

(c.) *The same regulations shall apply to the setting of Tombstones.*

119. *On the death of any Member of the Burial Society, or on any Member of that Society observing the week of mourning for a relative, and having* מנין, *one of the Readers or some other official of the congregation appointed for the purpose, shall, if required, read prayers at the house of mourning, evening or morning, as may be desired by the mourner, and shall, if required, deliver a discourse at least once during the week. The attendance of the Synagogue officials is limited to the house of mourning, or, failing that, to the house of the senior mourner— seniority implying seniority of Membership of the congregation.* Law of Burial Society.

120. *It shall be the duty of the Readers of the Constituent Synagogues to attend, when called upon, for the purpose of affording spiritual consolation to, and reading the appointed prayers with, the Seat-holders of their respective Synagogues, or members of the families of such Seatholders, when sick or dying.* Law of Burial Society.

121. *In the event of the Rabbi of the Burial* Bye-law of Council.

Ground being temporarily incapacitated from duty, one of the Readers of a Constituent Synagogue shall, on the requisition of the Treasurer for the time being of the Burial Society, be required to officiate in his stead.

122. *It shall be the duty of the Board of Management of each Constituent Synagogue to apportion among its ministers the performance of the duties prescribed in the laws of the Burial Society.*

123. The second Reader shall prepare the ספרי תורה and shall supervise the preparation of the vestments, ornaments, and everything requisite for the performance of the services in the Synagogue. If there be but one

In the West End Synagogue, this Bye-law reads as follows :— The Honorary Officers shall give directions to ensure the proper preparation of the ספרי תורה, *vestments, ornaments, and everything requisite for the performance of the service in the Synagogue.*

Reader, such duties shall be performed by him.

124. Any youth intending to read a פרשה upon the שבת of his being בר מצוה must give notice thereof, and must attend the Synagogue on a previous day, so that the Reader who officiates as בעל קורא (person appointed to read the תורה) may ascertain if he be competent to read such פרשה, and on the day of the youth's becoming בר מצוה the בעל קורא shall stand next to him during his reading of the פרשה.

125. Should any youth intending to read a פרשה on his becoming בר מצוה be found by the בעל קורא (person appointed to read the תורה) to be incompetent to read properly and to translate his פרשה, the בעל קורא shall report to the Presiding Warden, who shall have the power to withhold his permission for the youth to read.

126. The Reader who officiates as בעל קורא, or any

other person appointed to read the תורה, shall attend
the Synagogue on a day prior to every Sabbath or
Holyday, for the purpose of rehearsing the portion to
be read on such Sabbath or Holyday, and shall carefully
take note of any error that may be found by him in
the ספר תורה for the purpose of its correction.

127.   *The Readers shall also perform such other* Bye-law of Council.
clerical duties in this Synagogue, or in connection
with its Members, as shall be delegated to them by its
Wardens, and such other clerical duties as may be
specially delegated to them by the Council, or by any
of its Honorary Officers in their order of precedence.

SECRETARY.

128.   The Secretary shall be ex-officio a נאמן
(accredited Officer) of the Congregation.

129.   The Secretary shall keep the accounts of this
Synagogue, and shall take charge of all books,
documents and papers belonging thereto deposited
with him, and shall not show them to any one
(except to a Member of its Board of Management, or
to any of the Honorary Officers or to the Secretary
of the Council of the United Synagogue), without a
written order from the Warden President.

130.   *All cheques received by the Secretary of a* Bye-law of Council.
Constituent Synagogue shall be forthwith paid by
him to the Bankers of the United Synagogue to
the account thereof, and all other moneys received
by him (without such moneys being permitted to
accumulate beyond £30,) shall be paid to the said
Bankers to the like account.

131.   The Secretary shall issue all summonses

convening Meetings of the Board of Management, or
its Sub-Committees, and of the Members of the Synagogue, attend such Meetings, and take down the
minutes of their proceedings.

132. The Secretary shall attend the Meetings of
the Council and its Committees when required, and
shall perform such duties as the Council or its
Honorary Officers shall from time to time direct
or require.

133. The Secretary shall prepare the half-yearly
accounts for rental of seats and other moneys which
shall be due from the Members and Seatholders of this
Synagogue, shall conduct all its correspondence as
directed, communicate without delay to the Warden
President all matters relating to its business, and
perform all duties generally appertaining to the office
of Secretary.

134. The Secretary shall be the Registrar of
Marriages for this Synagogue, under the provisions
of the 6 & 7 Will. IV., c. 86. He shall attend the
solemnisation of Marriages, and register the same
in accordance with the provisions of the said Act,
and shall attest the כתובה (Marriage contract).

135. The Secretary shall also keep a record
of all marriages solemnized in connection with this
Synagogue which are not required, under 19 & 20
Vict., cap. 119, sec. 12, to be returned to the Regis-
trar-General, and shall attest the כתובה (Marriage
Contract).

136. The Secretary shall keep Registers of all
Births of Jewish children which are notified to
him for registration, and of all Marriages which are
attested by him under Bye-laws 134 and 135.

137. The Secretary shall keep a book, wherein shall be entered duplicate כתובות, which, previously to the solemnisation of a marriage, shall be signed by the same parties who sign the כתובה.

138. The Secretary shall receive a fee of 2s. 6d. for every Certificate of Birth, Marriage, or Burial given by him from the Registers, to be paid by the person requiring the same. But the Warden President shall have the power, on application, to order such certificate to be given without the payment of such fee.

139. All the property and effects belonging to or in the care of this Synagogue shall be in the charge of the Secretary, who shall be responsible for the safe custody of the same.

140. The Secretary shall prepare an Inventory in triplicate of all the property of this Synagogue for the use of its Financial Representative, in accordance with Bye-law 30.

141. The Secretary shall prepare the various forms and documents for the several Elections at this Synagogue, in accordance with the Laws and Bye-laws regulating the same.

142. The Secretary shall attend at the Office of this Synagogue at such times as may be fixed by the Board of Management.

At the Ham-bro', Boro', St. John's Wood and East London Syna-gogues, £200 instead of £500.   143. The Secretary, upon his appointment, shall find sureties to the satisfaction of the Board of Management of this Synagogue for an amount of not less than £500, and shall maintain such sureties to the satisfaction of that Board.

44

COLLECTOR.

144. All moneys due to this Synagogue shall be collected in such manner, at such time and by such Officer of the Synagogue as its Board of Management shall appoint. The collection shall be under the direction of the Financial Representative and Secretary, and subject to the control of the Board of Management.

145. All moneys received for the Synagogue by the Collector shall forthwith be handed over to the Secretary.

146. The Collector, upon his appointment shall find sureties to the satisfaction of the Board of Management to an amount of not less than £300, and shall maintain such sureties to the satisfaction of that Board.

At the Boro', St. John's Wood and East London Synagogues, £200 instead of £300.

BEADLE.

147. The Beadle shall open and close the Synagogue on every occasion when Divine Service is to be performed, or when any religious ceremonial is to take place therein, and shall remain in attendance in the Synagogue on all such occasions to maintain order.

In the Hambro' Synagogue many of these duties devolve upon the שמש.

148. The keys of the Synagogue shall be kept by the person residing thereat, and shall be delivered to such person by the Beadle upon his closing the Synagogue, unless the latter be the resident Officer, in which case he shall have them in his own custody.

149. The Beadle, under the direction of the Se- Vide Bye-law 123.
cretary, shall superintend the cleaning of the Synagogue, with its appurtenances, its plate and furniture,
shall keep the same in proper order for daily use, and
shall prepare the vestments, ornaments, and everything requisite for the performance of the service in
the Synagogue.

150. The Beadle shall be in attendance at all
Meetings of the Board of Management and of the
Members of this Synagogue, and at all Meetings of
the Council and its Committees held at this Synagogue.

151. The Beadle shall attend at the chambers of
this Synagogue on all occasions when the business of
the congregation shall require it; and shall perform
all duties required from him by the Officers of this
Synagogue, or of the United Synagogue.

152. The Beadle shall attend at any Marriage
Ceremony performed at or in connection with this
Synagogue, and shall convey and be responsible for
the care of the חופה.

GENERAL LAWS RESPECTING SALARIED OFFICERS.

153. *Salaried Officers in the service of the United* Bye-law of Council.
Synagogue, or of any of its Constituent Synagogues,
shall be exempt from the payment of Synagogue
taxes and charges for seats. If they shall be pos-
sessed of חזקת הקהלה *they shall retain all the rights*
of בעלי בתים *whilst holding office, except the right to*
vote on any occasion, and to be elected to, or to hold See Bye-law No. 105.
any honorary office.

154. A Salaried Officer of this Synagogue shall not absent himself from the performance of his duties without the previous permission of the Presiding Warden, which permission must also be obtained for any leave of absence.

155. No Salaried Officer who is a נאמן of the congregation shall be engaged in trade or business.

Sect. 61 of Schedule to United Synagogues Act, and Bye-law of Council.

156. *All Salaried Officers of the Constituent Synagogues shall ipso facto be deemed to be officers of the United Synagogue.*

Bye-law of Council.

157. *(a.) Upon a person being elected to serve any paid office in the United Synagogue, or any Constituent Synagogue thereof, he shall as a condition precedent to his entering upon the duties of such office, sign such agreement as to the performance of such duties, his tenure of office, and the salary attached thereto, and all matters incidental to such duties or office, as shall be determined on and required by the Executive Committee of the United Synagogue.*

(b.) Until such agreement shall have been signed and handed to the Secretary for the time being of the Council of the United Synagogue, the person elected shall not enter into office, nor shall any order for payment of money to him be honoured by the Treasurers of the United Synagogue.

(c.) Such agreement when handed over shall be retained among the archives of the United Synagogue.

(d.) The Wardens for the time being, or whoever may be the contracting party or parties on behalf of the United or Constituent Synagogue, shall in the happening of any breach or breaches of the agreement on the part of the officer, take all such steps for enforc-

ing the contract or terminating it as the Executive Committee of the United Synagogue shall from time to time direct or require.

SERVICE OF THE SYNAGOGUE.

158. *The form of worship in each of the Consti-* Clause 3, Deed of *tuent Synagogues, and all religious observances in the* Foundation *Constituent Synagogues, and all matters connected with* and Trust. *the religious administration of the United Synagogue, and of its subsidiary charities, shall, subject to the* . *provision in the scheme requiring such form of worship to be in accordance with the Polish or German ritual, be under the supervision and control of the Chief Rabbi.*

159. Subject to the provisions of Clause 3 of the Deed of Foundation and Trust of the United Synagogue, the superintendence of this Synagogue and the maintenance of order therein during the performance of Divine Service, shall be vested in the Warden President, or, in his absence, in the other Warden. If neither of these Officers be present, the duty of acting as Presiding Officer shall devolve in order of precedence on—

(*a.*) The Financial Representative.

(*b.*) Any Past Honorary Officer, being a Seat- See Clause 57, Schedule holder of this Synagogue, who at the United Syna- gogues Act. date of the passing of the United Synagogue Act was or had been an Honorary Officer of any Constituent Synagogue, according to his seniority of office.

(*c.*) Any member of the Board of Management according to seniority of membership of the United Synagogue.

(d.) Past Wardens of this Synagogue since the
date of the passing of the United Synagogues Act.

(e.) Representatives of this Synagogue at the
Council, according to seniority of membership of the United Synagogue.

(f.) The senior בית בעל present, who is a Seatholder in this Synagogue.

(g.) Seatholders in the order of seniority of their
tenure at any Constituent Synagogue.

160. The person upon whom the duty of presiding
in this Synagogue shall devolve, shall, for the time
being, be invested with all the authority of the
Warden President.

Clause 6,
Deed of
Foundation
and Trust.

161. *The Board of Management of a Constituent
Synagogue shall not, without the sanction of the Chief
Rabbi, permit any person to preach therein. No
person other than an accredited Officer of the United
Synagogue shall perform religious service at a Con-
stituent Synagogue, without the previous sanction
of the Board of Management thereof, and of the Chief
Rabbi.*

162. All proclamations made in the Synagogue relating to religious services or observances shall be in
the terms that may be directed by the Chief Rabbi,
and shall be sanctioned by the Presiding Honorary
Officer previously to being made therein.

163. The distribution of the מִצְוֹת during Divine
Service shall be made by the Presiding Officer in such
order and manner as the Board of Management may
from time to time determine; priority being given
to חיובים.

164. The Board of Management shall, subject to

the provisions of Cl. 3 of the Deed of Foundation and Trust, regulate the mode or precedence in which קדיש shall be said in the Synagogue by אבלים and persons observing יאהרצייט.

165. Seatholders, according to seniority, shall be permitted to read אשרי ובא לציון or מעריב בזמנו on the occasion of observing יאהרצייט or being אבל for a parent, precedence being given to a Seatholder observing יאהרצייט.

166. On הושענא רבא seven ספרי תורה shall be taken out of the Ark for the הקפות. The Presiding Officer shall take הוצאה והכנסה and the ספרים shall be presented in order to the following persons:—

(a.) The Warden;

(b.) The Financial Representative;

(c.) The חתן תורה and חתן בראשית;

(d.) Past Honorary Officers, being Seatholders of this Synagogue, who at the date of the passing of the United Synagogues Act were

or had been Honorary Officers of a Constituent Synagogue, according to their seniority of office;

(e.) Other persons in such order as the Board of Management may determine.

167. On שמחת תורה seven ספרים shall be taken out of the Ark, and shall be presented by the Presiding Officer in order to the following persons:—

(a.) חזן Reader;

(b.) The Chief Rabbi, Dayan or Preacher;

(c.) The חתן תורה and the חתן בראשית;

(d.) The persons in the order directed by Bye-law 166, Sub-sections a, b, c, d and e.

E

168. The Presiding Officer shall be סגן on every occasion when such office does not devolve by law upon a member.

169. A בעל בית, being a Seatholder, or a Seatholder in this Synagogue who shall have occupied a seat at a Constituent Synagogue for not less than one year immediately preceding, shall be entitled to officiate as סגן on the occasion of his son becoming בר מצוה; should the בר מצוה be an orphan, his nearest relative, being a בעל בית and Seatholder, or being a Seatholder in any of the Constituent Synagogues for not less than one year immediately preceding, shall be entitled to the same privilege.

170. On the Sabbath previous to the celebration of a Marriage, when the bridegroom is called to the reading of the Law, the father of the bride or bridegroom, provided he be a בעל בית and Seatholder, or a Seatholder who shall have occupied a seat at this or any other Constituent Synagogue for not less than one year immediately preceding, shall have the privilege of officiating as סגן. In the event of the father being dead, then the nearest relative of the bride or bridegroom, such relative being a בעל בית and Seatholder, or a Seatholder who shall have occupied a seat at this or any other Constituent Synagogue for not less than one year immediately preceding, shall have the like privilege.

171. Should several of the cases specified in Byelaws 169 and 170 occur on the same Sabbath, the privilege of officiating as סגן shall devolve upon that person of those entitled to such privilege, who is the senior בעל בית or Seatholder; the parent of the בר מצוה, bride, or bridegroom, as the case may be, having the preference over any other relative, and in all

such cases an Honorary Officer shall have the right
of priority; and Seatholders in this Synagogue shall
have the right of priority over Seatholders in any
other Constituent Synagogue.

172.   On the Sabbath after the annual election of the
Honorary Officers and Board of Management of this
Synagogue, a מי שברך shall be made in the Syna-
gogue after the reading of the Law, in which the
names of such Officers and of the Members of the
Board for the ensuing year shall be proclaimed.

173.   On יום כפור and on מתנת יד the prayer of
אל מלא רחמים shall be said, and a general הזכרה
without names shall be made for all persons who
have bequeathed money or other property to the
United Synagogue, or to any of its subsidiary Charities, or to any of its Constituent Synagogues.

In Bayswater and West End Synagogues the record of past offerings is read once a year, only (ליל יום כפור). In the Boro' Synagogue past bequests of £2 2s. to the Local, or future bequests of £5 5s. to the General Funds are to be inscribed on the memorial list.

174.   On ליל יום כפור preceding the
Evening Service (מעריב), on the seventh
night of פסח, the night of שמיני עצרת,
and the first night of שבועות (except
when such shall occur on Saturday evening), immediately after the Afternoon
Service (תפלת מנחה), a list shall be read
of the names of all persons, having been
Seatholders of this Synagogue, who have
died and bequeathed the sum of £10 or
upwards to the United Synagogue, or to
any of its subsidiary Charities, or to any
of its Constituent Synagogues. The names of persons
not Seatholders, who have bequeathed money to the
Congregation, shall be announced in such Constituent
Synagogue as the Council shall direct. Should
ערב שבועות happen on שבת, the same course shall be
adopted on the second evening of שבועות before the
commencement of the Evening Service.

E 2

175. When אבלים attend the Synagogue on any
Friday evening, their presence shall be announced,
and they shall be received at the entrance of the
Synagogue by the Chief Rabbi (if present) and the
חונים Readers.

CALLING OF PERSONS TO THE READING OF THE LAW AND OFFERINGS.

See Bye-law 6.

176. The order of precedence in קריאת התורה
(being called to the reading of the law) shall be as
follows :

(*a.*) The Chief Rabbi;

(*b.*) The Wardens ;

(*c.*) The Financial Representative;

See Clause 57 of Schedule to the United Synagogues Act.

(*d.*) Past Honorary Officers, being Seatholders of
this Synagogue, who, at the date of the
passing of the United Synagogues Act,
were or had been Honorary Officers of a
Constituent Synagogue, according to their
seniority of office;

(*e.*) Members of the Board of Management ;

(*f.*) Past Honorary Officers of this Synagogue
having held office since the date of the passing of the United Synagogues Act, being
Seatholders in this Synagogue;

(*g.*) Representatives of this Synagogue at the
Council of the United Synagogue;

(*h.*) בעלי בתים being Seatholders according to
their registered seniority of Privileged
Membership;

(*i.*) Seatholders in this Synagogue according to
the registered seniority of their continuous

tenure of a seat in any of the Constituent Synagogues.

177. The Wardens shall direct the formation of a list of persons to be invited in rotation לקריאת התורה to the reading of the Law in the order contained in Bye-law 176.

178. The Secretary shall forward a notice to each person on the list, apprising him of the day fixed for his being called to the reading of the Law, commencing on ראש השנה and proceeding according to the order of the list until פסח. Should the list not be exhausted by פסח it shall be recommenced and continued until the end of the list of Members comprised in the first seven Sub-sections of Bye-law 176, after which it shall be resumed where it was previously terminated.

179. The rotation provided for in Bye-law 176 shall be superseded on the occasion of the calling to the Law of the following persons, who are חיובים :—

(a.) A boy, on becoming בר מצוה;

(b.) A bridegroom on the שבת previous to his marriage.

(c.) The father or nearest male relation of a בר מצוה boy;

(d.) A husband on his wife's returning thanks after childbirth;

(e.) A person on the day of his יאהרצייט;

(f.) A בעל ברית;

(g.) A סנדק;

(h.) A person desirous of returning thanks ברכת הגומל on recovery from sickness, or escaping from danger, or returning from a journey.

The rotation may also be superseded by the Presiding Officer, to permit the relatives of any of the above, or any visitor, or any person attending the Synagogue, being called to the Law.

180. חיובים shall not have any prior right to be called to the reading of the Law on the following days and times; ימים טובים, מנחה בשבת, חול המועד, ימים נוראים and יום ב' וה', (except as to persons on the day of their יאהרצייט on יום ב' וה'), but they may be called to the Law on those days with the permission of the Presiding Officer.

181. Any person being a חיוב shall give notice thereof to the Secretary on or before the Thursday preceding the שבת upon which he is to be called to the reading of the Law, and the Secretary shall communicate the same to the Warden President. In the event of the said person being twelve months or more in arrear of payment of his account to the Synagogue, the Warden President, in conjunction with the Financial Representative, shall decide whether and upon what terms of payment such person shall be permitted to exercise the rights of a חיוב or of סגן.

182. The Chief Rabbi is a חיוב on the following days :—the שבת previous to every ראש חדש, the first days of פסח שבועות וראש השנה, and on שבת הגדול and שבת שובה, שבת חזי, שמחת תורה.

183. Persons called to the reading of the Law shall only be permitted to make a מי שברך in such manner as the Board of Management shall determine.

184. Any person, with the permission of the Presiding Officer, may make a special offering by means of a מי שברך without being called to the reading of the

Law; such offering shall be declared in the Synagogue at such period of the Service and in such manner as the Board of Management shall determine.

חתן תורה and חתן בראשית

185. A Meeting of the Board of Management shall be held annually in or about the latter part of the month of Ellul, at which eight persons shall be selected by them from a list of the Seatholders in this Synagogue, and the two Seatholders having the highest number of votes shall be declared duly elected to the offices of חתן תורה and חתן בראשית.

186. In the event of one or more of such persons declining to fill such offices, the next in rotation having the highest number of votes shall be deemed duly elected thereto. The names of the persons accepting such offices shall be announced in the Synagogue on the first day of סכות.

187. In the event of all the persons who may be elected for the office of חתן תורה, or of חתן בראשית, declining to serve, it shall devolve upon the Honorary Officers to fill the same.

188. The חתן בראשית and תן התורה shall attend the Synagogue on שמהת תורה and שבת בראשית to be called to the reading of the Law, and during the service they shall be seated in the Wardens' box.

MARRIAGES.

189. No Marriage shall be solemnised in connection with this Synagogue, without the written authorisation of the Chief Rabbi.

190. The Chief Rabbi's Certificate, authorising the solemnisation of the Marriage, together with the Superintendent Registrar's Certificate of the notice of Marriage (given by such Registrar in accordance Vide 19 and 20 Vict., c. 119, Secs. 4 and 9. with the provisions of the 19 and 20 Vict., c. 119, Sec. 4), shall be delivered to the Secretary of this Synagogue by or on behalf of the parties contracting to marry, and if possible shall be left with him at least seven days previously to the intended solemnisation of the Marriage. If such Marriage is to be solemnised by license, then the Chief Rabbi's Certificate, and the Superintendent Registrar's Certificate (given under Sec. 9 of the before-mentioned Act), shall be left with the Secretary of this Synagogue as soon as they shall have been obtained.

191. In the event of a Bridegroom being in arrear of payment of his account due to this Synagogue, the Warden President, in conjunction with the Financial Representative, shall decide whether, and upon what terms of payment such person shall be permitted to have the Marriage ceremony performed at or in connection with this Synagogue.

Bye-law of Council.

192. *No person shall be permitted to have the ceremony of marriage solemnised at or in connection with a Constituent Synagogue who is indebted to any other of the Constituent Synagogues, without the consent of the Honorary Officers of the Synagogue to which the debt is owing.*

Bye-law of Council.

193. *The special permission of the Chief Rabbi shall be required to authorise any officer of a Constituent Synagogue to solemnise marriages.*

Bye-law of Council.

194. *The Marriage ceremony of any seatholder of a Constituent Synagogue, or of any person desirous of being married in connection with such Synagogue,*

shall, subject to the provisions of Bye-law 196, *be solemnised by the Preacher or one of the Readers of the Constituent Synagogue of which the bridegroom is a seatholder, or of which he by marriage becomes a member.*

195. *The following fees and charges shall be paid* Bye-law of
Council. *for the solemnisation of a Marriage at or in connection with the Synagogue :—*

The Chief Rabbi	.	.	.	£1	1	0
Consolidated Charges	.	.	2	2	0
When the Ceremony is not solemnised in the Synagogue or in the Synagogue Chambers, exclusive of cab fares	.	2	0	0

When the ceremony is solemnised at a distance beyond the radius of ten miles from the Constituent Synagogue in connection with which it is registered, a further charge of £2 2s. shall be made in addition to the above charges, which sum of £2 2s. shall be divided among the officers attending such marriage in such proportion as the Wardens of the Constituent Synagogue shall determine.

196. *(a.) Should any member of a Constituent* Bye-law of
Council. *Synagogue, or person who by marriage becomes a member of a Constituent Synagogue, desire to have his marriage solemnised by a Preacher or Reader of the United Synagogue other than the Preacher or Reader of such Constituent Synagogue, he shall make application for the purpose, at least fifteen days before the date of the marriage, to the Secretary of the United Synagogue at the office of the same.*

(b.) The Preacher or Reader whose services are required under the previous sub-section for the solemnisation of a marriage, shall, on receiving an intimation to that effect from the Secretary of the

United Synagogue, comply with such request; and if there be more than one application for his services on the same day and hour, then he shall comply with such requests in the order of priority of application; provided always that due regard be had by him to the prior right of members, or of persons who by marriage become members, of his own special Synagogue, who shall have a preferential claim to his services over persons desirous of availing themselves thereof under Sub-Section a.

(c.) The right of choosing a Preacher or Reader for the celebration of the marriage of a member, or of a person who becomes a member, of a Constituent Synagogue, other than the Minister of such Constituent Synagogue, is limited to the choice of such Preachers or Readers as are not at the same time official Registrars of Marriages.

(d.) All applications to the Secretary of the United Synagogue, in accordance with Sub-Section a, for the services of a Preacher or Reader as the celebrant of a marriage, shall be accompanied by a payment of £3 3s. to the funds of the United Synagogue, which sum shall be returned in the event of the services of such Preacher or Reader not being procured. The said sum of £3 3s. is exclusive of, and in addition to, the Marriage Charges enumerated in Bye-Law 195.

(e.) From the said amount of £3 3s. the sum of £1 1s. shall be allowed in lieu of expenses to the Preacher or Reader officiating at the marriages of persons other than members, or persons becoming members, of his own Synagogue.

Bye-law of Council.

197. (a.) Persons desiring to be married at a lower rate than that specified in Bye-law 195, shall be entitled to claim the right of being married for the sum of 10s. 6d.

(b.) Marriages celebrated under the conditions of Section a of this Bye-law, shall be solemnised at one of the so-called minor Synagogues.

(c.) In the case of the marriage of Seatholders of any of the Constituent Synagogues, or of their children, or of persons who may have at any time been contributing Seatholders for any period amounting in the whole to two years, or of their children, a power of reduction or remission of the larger fee (specified in Bye-law 195) shall be vested in any two of the Honorary Officers of that Synagogue, the Marriage to take place in the Synagogue of which the bridegroom is or becomes a member in the same manner as if the fees had not been reduced or remitted. Every application for such reduction or remission to be made on a form of application to be provided for the purpose, and to be submitted by the Secretary of this Synagogue to his Honorary Officers for decision.

(d.) A similar power of remission of the smaller fee (specified in Section a of this Bye-law) shall be vested in the Overseers of the United Synagogue, with respect to marriages solemnised in one of the minor Synagogues, the marriage to take place there in the same manner as if the fee had not been remitted. Every application for such remission to be made on a form of application to be provided for the purpose, and to be addressed to the Secretary of the United Synagogue, who shall submit it to the Overseers for their decision.

(e.) The Marriages celebrated at one of the minor Synagogues, under Sections a, b, and d of this Bye-law, shall be solemnised by such one of the accredited Ministers of the Constituent Synagogues, and registered by such one of its Secretaries, or in such rotation, as the Executive Committee of the United

Synagogue may from time to time determine; but persons marrying at one of the minor Synagogues shall not be entitled to avail themselves for the celebration of marriage of the services of a Preacher or Reader other than the officers of the Synagogue in connection with which the marriage is registered.

Bye-law of Council.

198. All fees and charges payable upon the performance of a Marriage ceremony in connection with this Synagogue shall be collected by the Secretary previously to the solemnisation thereof.

199. *The amount of the wedding charges (except the charge payable under Bye-law 196 d) shall be received as at present by the Constituent Synagogue in connection with which the marriage is registered, and such charges, except the fee payable to the Chief Rabbi, shall be paid into the Cash account of the Synagogue.*

Bye-law of Council.

200. *All Marriages not solemnised at the private residences of either of the persons married, or in rooms provided by them, shall be solemnised, without distinction whatever of place, in the Synagogue, unless prevented by the actual performance therein of Divine Service, or by the Synagogue being under repair, or by the Marriage having been inadvertently registered to take place at the Synagogue Chambers.*

Bye-law of Council.

201. *Full publicity shall be given, in such manner as the Executive Committee may from time to time deem advisable, to the regulations under which marriages may in future be solemnised at various rates,*

BOARD OF MANAGEMENT TO MAKE BYE-LAWS.

202.   *The Board of Management of a Constituent*
Sec. 52, Schedule to United Syna- gogues Act.

Synagogue may make and submit to the Council Bye- laws for the regulation and management of matters of a local nature affecting the same Constituent Synagogue, and such Bye-laws shall be considered by the Council, and shall take effect, if and so far as the same shall be confirmed, and subject to any variations which may be made by the Council, provided that no such Bye-laws are repugnant to or inconsistent with this scheme or the Bye-laws of the United Synagogue for the time being in force.

REPEAL OF OLD LAWS.

203.   *The foregoing Bye-laws shall commence and* Bye-law of Council.

take effect from the date of the Meeting of Council confirming the same (כ"ח חשון תרמ"א *November 2nd, 1880), and thereupon all the old Laws and Regulations of this Synagogue shall be and are hereby repealed in accordance with the provisions of Sec. 52 of the Schedule to the United Synagogues Act.*

EXTRACTS from ACTS of PARLIAMENT
REGULATING MARRIAGES.

6 and 7 Will. IV., c. 85, Extract from Sec. 2.

Persons professing the Jewish religion may continue to contract and solemnise Marriages according to the usages of the said persons respectively; and every such Marriage is hereby declared and confirmed good in law, provided that the parties to such Marriage be both persons professing the Jewish religion respectively; provided also that notice to the Registrar shall have been given and the Registrar's certificate shall have been issued in manner hereinafter provided.

6 and 7 Will. IV., c. 85, Extract from Sec. 4.

Vide 19 and 20 Vict., c. 119, Sec. 3.

In every case of marriage intended to be solemnised in England according to the usages of the Jews, one of the parties shall give notice under his or her hand in the form (contained in the schedule annexed to 19 and 20 Vict., c. 119, sec. 3) to the Superintendent Registrar of the district within which the parties shall have dwelt for not less than seven days then next preceding, or if the parties dwell in the districts of different Superintendent Registrars, shall give the like notice to the Superintendent Registrar of each district, and shall state therein the names and surnames, and the profession or condition of each of the parties intending Marriage, the dwelling place of each of them, and the time, not being less than seven days, during which each has dwelt therein, and the building in which the Marriage is to be solemnised; provided that if either party shall have dwelt in the place stated in the notice during more than one calendar month, it may be stated therein that he or she hath dwelt there one month and upwards.

Any marriages according to the usages of persons professing the Jewish religion, where the parties thereto are both persons professing the Jewish religion, may be solemnised by license (which license the Superintendent Registrar to whom notice of the intended Marriage shall have been given is authorised to grant) as effectually in all respects as if such Marriage were solemnised after the issue of a certificate by such Superintendent Registrar. 19 and 20 Vict. c. 119, Extract from Sec. 21.

The Registrar-General shall furnish or cause to be furnished to every person whom the President for the time being of the London Committee of Deputies of the British Jews shall from time to time certify in writing under his hand to the Registrar-General to be the Secretary of a Synagogue in England of persons professing the Jewish religion, a sufficient number in duplicate of Marriage Register Books, and Forms for certified copies thereof. 6 and 7 Will. IV., c. 86, Extract from Sec. 30.

Every Secretary of a Synagogue, immediately after every Marriage solemnised between any two persons professing the Jewish religion, of whom the husband shall belong to the Synagogue whereof he is Secretary, shall register, or cause to be registered, in duplicate, in two of the said Marriage Register Books, the several particulars relating to that marriage, according to the form of the schedule (annexed to the Act), and every such Secretary, whether he shall or shall not be present at such marriage, shall satisfy himself that the proceedings in relation thereto have been conformable to the 6 and 7 Will. IV., c. 86, Extract from Sec. 31.

usages of the persons professing the Jewish religion,
and every such entry as hereinbefore is mentioned
(made by such Secretary as aforesaid), shall be signed
by the said Secretary, and by the parties married, and
by two witnesses, and shall be made in order, from
the beginning to the end of each book; and the number
of the place of entry in each duplicate Marriage Register
Book shall be the same.

G and 7 Will.
IV., c. 86,
Extract from
Sec. 33.

Every Secretary shall, in the months of April,
July, October, and January, respectively, make and
deliver to the Superintendent Registrar of the district
which may be assigned by the Registrar-General
to such Secretary, on durable materials, a true copy,
certified by him under his hand, of all the entries
of Marriages in the Register Book kept by him since the
last certificate, and to contain all the entries made up to
that time;* and if there shall have been no Marriage
entered therein since the last certificate, shall certify
the fact under his hand, and shall keep the said
Marriage Register Books safely until the same shall
be filled; and one copy of every such Register Book,
when filled, shall be delivered to the Superintendent
Registrar of the district which shall have been assigned
to such Secretary; and the other copy of every such
Register Book of Marriages among persons professing the Jewish religion shall remain under the care
of the said persons, to be kept with their other registers
and records, and shall for the purposes of this Act
be still deemed to be in the keeping of the Secretary
for the time being.†

* By 1 Vict., c. 22, sec. 6, the certified copies are to be made up and to refer
respectively to the last days of March, June, September, and December then
next preceding.

† By 1 Vict., c. 22, sec. 28, neglect to comply with the provisions of the
33rd sec. of 6 and 7 Will. IV., c. 86, subjects the offender to a penalty of £10.

INDEX.

—o—

F

CLAUSE